ORGANIZATION DEVELOPMENT:
STRATEGIES AND MODELS

RICHARD BECKHARD
Richard Beckhard Associates, New York
and
Massachusetts Institute of Technology

ADDISON-WESLEY PUBLISHING COMPANY
Reading, Massachusetts · Menlo Park, California
London · Amsterdam · Don Mills, Ontario · Sydney

This book is in the Addison-Wesley series:

ORGANIZATION DEVELOPMENT

Editors
Edgar Schein
Warren Bennis
Richard Beckhard

To LEE, who lived through it,
with gratitude and love.

ISBN 0-201-00448-8
VWXYZ-MU-8943210

FOREWORD

The purpose of this common foreword to all the volumes of the Addison-Wesley Series on Organization Development is twofold: (1) to give the reader some idea as to the origin and purpose of the series; and (2) to guide the reader through the content of the different books.

The series came to be because we felt there was a growing theory and practice of something called "organization development," but most students, colleagues, and managers knew relatively little about it. Many of us are highly active as OD consultants, but little has been written about what we do when we are with a client or what our underlying theory of consultation is. We were also acutely aware of the fact that, though there are common assumptions shared by most practitioners of OD, there are great individual variations in the strategies and tactics employed by different consultants. The field is still emerging and new methods are constantly being invented. It seemed appropriate, therefore, not to try to write a single text, but to give several of the foremost theorist-practitioners a chance to explain their own view of OD and their own style of working with client systems.

The authors of this series of six books represent a variety of points of view, but they do not exhaust the major approaches currently in use in OD. There are some obvious names missing—Argyris, Tannenbaum, Ferguson, Bradford, Davis, Burke—to name just a few. We hope in future volumes of the series to get these men and others to write about their theory and practice.

The six books of this series can be described as follows: Bennis presents a very broad survey of the history and present practice of OD. How and why did it come about, what is it, and what are some of the major unresolved issues in OD? The Beckhard volume is a systematic attempt to describe the various strategies and tactics employed in different kinds of OD efforts. Beckhard goes beyond his own approach and tries to build a general framework within which most OD programs can be located. The Beckhard and Bennis volumes together give the reader an excellent overview of the field.

The two volumes by Blake and Mouton and by Lawrence and Lorsch are somewhat more personalized statements of their particular views of how organizations function, how organizational excellence is to be judged, and how an OD effort can contribute to the achievement of such excellence. Both books are focused on total organization systems and attempt to show how intervention in organizations leads to constructive change and development.

The volumes by Walton and Schein are written at a more specific level. They highlight some of the day-to-day activities of the consultant as he works with a client system in the context of an OD program. Both deal with the process of the consultation itself. In the Walton book the focus is on the process by which the consultant uses himself to aid in the resolution of conflict. In the Schein book the idea of "process consultation" is introduced and explained in detail. The kinds of organizational processes which are described in these last two volumes lie at the heart of OD efforts, but the focus of the books is on the moment-to-moment behavior of the consultant rather than the overall design of the OD program.

The six books are written independently with only broad guidelines and minimum coordination by the editors. It was our hope and intention to get six very personal and unique statements, rather than a closely integrated set of "chapters." We feel that the amount of overlap is minimal, and that the books in fact complement each other very well in being written at different levels of generality. We hope that the reader will sense that the field of OD is converging toward common theories and practices, but that we are a long way from being able to produce a definitive "text" on the subject.

March 1969   Edgar H. Schein
                                                        Richard Beckhard
                                                        Warren G. Bennis

PREFACE

Enterprise managers today are deeply concerned with the dilemma of how to (a) fully mobilize the energy of the organization's human resources toward achievement of the organization's performance objectives, and (b) at the same time, so organize the work, the work environment, the communications systems, and the relationships of people, that individuals' needs for self worth, growth, and satisfaction are significantly met at work.

To resolve this dilemma in our rapidly changing environment, new organization forms must be developed; more effective goal-setting and planning processes must be learned, and practiced teams of interdependent people must spend real time improving their methods of working, decision-making, and communicating. Competing or conflicting groups must move toward a collaborative way of work. In order for these changes to occur and be maintained, a *planned*, managed change effort is necessary—a program of *organization development*.

This book, written for managers, specialists, and students of management who are concerned with the planning and conduct of such programs, is based largely on the author's own experience in helping organization leaders with planned-change efforts, and on related experience of colleagues in the field. The organization of the material is as follows:

Chapter 1 presents the background and causes for the increased concern with organization development and planned change. It explores the various themes of such improvement efforts over the past half-century.

v

Chapter 2 defines organization development as a phenomenon, and then compares and relates it to management development, training, and operations research.

Chapter 3 reviews and describes the types of strategies, tactics, and activities that are used in organization-development efforts.

The next five chapters are actual cases of organizationwide, planned-change efforts. Each case represents a specific change-target emphasis. *Chapter 4* is a change in the "culture" of the organization; *Chapter 5,* a change in managerial strategy; *Chapter 6,* a change in the way work is organized; *Chapter 7,* the creative adaptation to a new environment, and *Chapter 8,* changes in influence and communication patterns.

Chapter 9 analyzes the conditions and characteristics of successful and unsuccessful organization-development efforts.

Chapter 10 is concerned with the *management* of organization development—it looks at different strategies of managing. It also describes the different types of outside help used by organizations in OD efforts. Finally, it describes different methods of organizing the specialist effort inside the organization.

The last chapter looks briefly ahead to what we might expect as major influences in the field of organization improvement in the next decade.

My intent in writing this book has been to provide a relatively systematic description of the "state of the art," and to give the reader some criteria on the basis of which he can make decisions on the planning and conduct of organization-development programs and activities. To the degree that it does this, it will have served its purpose.

I am grateful to so many people for their help that I will make no attempt to list them all. I must, however, express special thanks to my colleague, Ed Schein, for his encouragement, criticism, and help; to my wife, Lee, who read, questioned, supported, and transported manuscript; and to my secretary, Harriet Stanton, who typed, retyped, and decoded my illegible script and turned it into manuscript.

Cambridge, Mass.   R.B.
January 1969

CONTENTS

PART 1

THE 'WHAT,' 'WHY,' AND 'HOW'
OF ORGANIZATION DEVELOPMENT

1

THE CHANGING ENVIRONMENT OF CHANGE

A universal preoccupation of enterprise managers is to develop and adapt their organizations to better cope with and shape the environment in which the enterprise operates. "Productivity" and "motivation" are two words inevitably linked.

Throughout this century, the efforts of managers to cope with and shape their environments, through the way they organize and operate their enterprises, have followed certain identifiable themes.

The major theme during the first third of the century was the attempt, through better "human engineering," to rationalize the way work was done; the way the work force was utilized to increase the output; and the productivity of the goods and services produced. This theme reached its peak during the Second World War.

After World War II, with the considerably improved human condition, working men began to demand that the work environment meet some of their social needs in addition to needs for survival and security. This impelled management to enter into a major search for a strategy to meet this new requirement. We saw the emergence, therefore, of a second theme: the "human relations" approach, where the focus was on man's social needs and ways of meeting them to increase motivation and organization productivity.

This theme continued into the Fifties. In the late Fifties and early Sixties, a new theme emerged for developing people for higher responsibilities. Improvements in benefit programs, an increase in mandatory retirements, and the rapid expansion of management requirements, in addition to rapid organization expansion, all intensified the need for planned management succession and development programs.

A second theme emerged from the resultant increasing complexities of organizations. Decentralization of decision-making, the growth of sophisticated computers with their new language, and geographic expansion, all combined to require managerial attention to the development of more effective information systems.

In the mid-Sixties, the theme changes again. A new one is developing focused on "total-system" change along a variety of dimensions. This theme focuses on *system examination*—looking at the organization as a complex, human system with a unique character, its own culture, and a value system. This character, the culture, and the values, as well as the information systems and work procedures, must be continually examined, analyzed, and improved if optimum productivity and motivation are to result.

The theme is stated in terms of the dilemma described in the *Preface:* How can we optimally mobilize human resources and energy to achieve the organization's mission and, at the same time, maintain a viable, growing organization of people whose personal needs for self worth, growth, and satisfaction are significantly met at work?

NEW ENVIRONMENTS

Today's Dynamic World

Management today operates in a very different environment than ever before. First, the general environment is *highly dynamic*. The Sixties may well be described as the "decade of the explosion." We list below a few examples of the phenomenon.

1. *The Knowledge Explosion.* More new knowledge in technology has been developed in the last ten years than in the history of mankind.

2. *The Technological Explosion.* Due to the increase in technological knowledge and sophistication, it has been estimated that most scientists are technically obsolete ten years after graduation from a technical graduate school. Not only do they lack the latest in their own technology but they may well be unfamiliar with the ten or fifteen new sciences and technologies which have sprung up in the meantime. It's a sobering fact to realize that 93 percent of all scientists who ever lived are alive today.

3. *The Communications Explosion.* Shortened distances make it quite possible to travel back and forth across an ocean in a few hours. Shortened communications lines make it possible to have a videophone conference with people around the world. Instant news on television affects all policy and planning.

4. *The Economic Explosion.* The changing nature of the work force is a very important factor. The worker in Western countries is no longer dependent upon a particular firm for employment. There are choices. Because of this he is in a position to ask for a greater share of the rewards and the profits. It is a fact in the United States, at the time of this writing, that practically every employable person has a choice of more than one place to work. Such a condition makes entirely different demands on management and the work force and sets up entirely new relationships between them.

Another change in the nature of the work force is the increase in *professionalism.* Today, company loyalty is, in large segments of organizations, being replaced by professional loyalty. Today's engineer or computer specialist or personnel specialist is a member of a *fraternity of specialists* representing a common technology. His membership in this society tends to be more central to him than his membership in a particular organization. The implications of this for rewards systems, recruiting, and training, are formidable.

Another condition which pertains in work forces throughout the world is that we are in the midst of a revolution of "class structure." Social class is more and more being replaced by economic class. More and more people see the opportunity of moving out of the subsistence category and toward a condition in which they can lead a more dignified life. This means that the consequences of managerial acts are quite different. The need for dialogue, for example, between members of junior management and members of the work force, is much greater today than when each stayed in his own class compartment and communicated only in terms of work tasks.

Today's Business Environment

In addition to the dynamic *general* environment, the *business environment* is also different from all past experience. Let me list just a few of the changes going on today.

1. *The Internationalization of Markets.* One organizes quite differently if one has the posture of an American company which does business

"abroad" than if the posture is that of a world-wide enterprise with a headquarters in America. In the latter mode, for example, you wouldn't have an international division.

2. *Shorter Product Life.* Location of plants as related to markets, and the size and flexibility of facilities are all becoming increasingly complex choices. Even where "planned obsolescence" is not a design feature, the fickleness of the public taste and the need to meet sharp competition demand continuing reassessment of production and distribution facilities.

3. *Increasing Significance of Marketing.* The change from production-oriented organizations to technical and marketing-oriented organizations means that different people are closer to the centers of influence in the organization. The power relationships change. The problems of managing technology and managing a sophisticated marketing approach are very different from those involved in managing a production organization.

4. *Relationship of Line and Staff.* New business, market, and organization requirements and the emergence of automation and sophisticated information systems have resulted in significant changes in the balance of numbers of "staff" and "line" people required. It seems clear that, in the foreseeable future, staff functions will considerably outnumber line operating functions. As a matter of fact, there is some danger of creating a new "establishment"—the *establishment of the specialists.* In this, the control of the enterprise might be spread among a number of experts, with the management providing administrative coordination.

5. *Multiple Memberships.* New businesses, products, and technologies require new or different structures and forms to achieve their goals. For example, it is impossible to assemble a new spaceship requiring the combined efforts of over 100,000 people scattered throughout the country, in the same way or within the same "pyramid" structure that would work for assembling an automobile in one plant.

Changing requirements are producing a variety of new forms such as temporary systems or an interdependent matrix organization with program management on one side of the matrix and capabilities on the other.

These new organization forms require people to belong to several groups; to have several bosses; to cope with competition for their time and energy from different programs. This means a greater requirement for interpersonal competence to handle these situations; for tolerance of the increased ambiguity; for expanded decision-making and planning capability.

6. *The Changing Nature of Work.* Increased or advanced technology means that machines not only make *products* that men used to make, but make *decisions* that men used to make. The management job becomes one of knowing what types of decisions should be made by man and by machine. This produces a whole new set of demands on the manager.

Today's Changing Values

Perhaps even more important than the dynamic general environment and the changing business environment is a third condition: changing values. Many values are changing dramatically as the human condition improves. Let me list a few that I believe are relatively universal today and that have great implications for managerial strategy.

1. Man is and *should* be more independent/autonomous.

2. Man has and *should* have *choices* in his work and in his leisure.

3. Security needs should be met. Man should be striving to meet higher-order needs for self worth and for realizing his own potential.

4. If man's individual needs are in conflict with organization requirements, he may and perhaps *should choose* to meet his own needs rather than submerge them in the organization requirements.

5. The organization should so organize work that tasks are meaningful and stimulating, and thus provide intrinsic rewards plus adequate extrinsic (money) rewards.

6. The power previously vested in bosses is reduced and should be. With choices in work and leisure, managers should manage by influence (appropriate behavior), rather than through force or the giving or withholding of financial rewards.

NEW KNOWLEDGE

During the past twenty years, from research in the social sciences and particularly in the behavioral sciences, there has emerged a good deal of new knowledge about the nature of human nature, the nature of organizations, and the nature of management. Readers of this book may be acquainted with Douglas McGregor's Theory X and Theory Y[1] in which

---

1   McGregor, D. *The Human Side of Enterprise.* New York: McGraw-Hill, 1960.

he looks at the implications for different managerial strategies, of different assumptions about the nature of people. Readers will probably also be familiar with Rensis Likert's analysis of organization systems[2] and may know his work in defining systems as either exploitive-authoritative, or benevolent-authoritative, or consultative, or participative. Readers will probably be familiar with Blake and Mouton's Managerial Grid[3,4] and the kind of organization climate conditions and structure that they see as relevant to the changing environment.

New forms of organizations such as the matrix organization referred to previously, which is used by many technology-oriented institutions and government organizations, are but an illustration of the applications of new knowledge to the organization of work.

NEW MANAGERIAL STRATEGIES

Most progressive managers today are deeply concerned with the problem of developing managerial strategies appropriate to the changing conditions. The word "change" is no longer even a buzz word. It has become part of our everyday language. Managers are continually working on the problems of how to develop a flexible organization which can move with changing requirements, which can be "proactive" (influencing the environment) rather than reactive. Managers are seeking ways to establish a work climate in which increasingly complex decisions can be made by people *with the information* regardless of their location in the organization. Managers are looking for ways in which increasingly complex technologies can be managed and in which people who have an ever higher sense of freedom and autonomy can be encouraged to *want* to stay and work in their organizations. The search for ways of concurrently increasing collaboration among the members of organizations and at the same time increasing the rationality of decisions occupies many hours of management time and many chapters in management books.

Organization development is the name that is being attached to *total-system,* planned-change efforts for coping with the above-mentioned conditions.

2   Likert, R. *The Human Organization.* New York: McGraw-Hill, 1967.
3   Blake, R. R., and J. S. Mouton. *The Managerial Grid.* Houston: Gulf Publishing Co., 1964.
4   Blake, R. R., and J. S. Mouton. *Corporate Excellence through Grid Organization Development.* Houston: Gulf Publishing Co., 1968.

In the last few years, more and more organization leaders have realized that it is not enough to carry out piecemeal efforts to patch up an organization problem here, fix a procedure there, or change a job description. Today, there is a need for longer-range, coordinated strategy to develop organization climates, ways of work, relationships, communications systems, and information systems that will be congruent with the predictable and unpredictable requirements of the years ahead. It is out of these needs that systematic planned-change efforts—organization development—have emerged.

In the following chapters we shall explore this phenomenon of organization development, examine some strategies that are being employed in organizations today, and discuss some implications for the future.

2

ORGANIZATION DEVELOPMENT:
PLANNED ENVIRONMENT CHANGE

I want to look now at *organization development* as a phenomenon. In this chapter, I will first develop an operational definition of organization development, or OD, as it is usually called. I will examine the characteristics of an effective and healthy organization, then look at the operational goals of organization-development efforts, and discuss some of the generalizable characteristics of organization-development efforts. I will then examine some types of organization conditions that produce such a planned-change effort. Finally, I will compare organization-development efforts with other planned-change efforts such as management-development programs, organization-wide training efforts, and operations-research efforts.

WHAT IS ORGANIZATION DEVELOPMENT?

Definition. Organization development is an effort (1) *planned,* (2) *organization-wide,* and (3) *managed* from the *top,* to (4) increase *organization effectiveness* and *health* through (5) *planned interventions* in the organization's "processes," using *behavioral-science* knowledge.

1. It is a *planned change* effort.

An OD program involves a systematic diagnosis of the organization, the development of a strategic plan for improvement, and the mobilization of resources to carry out the effort.

9

2. It involves the total *"system."*

An organization-development effort is related to a total organization change such as a change in the culture or the reward systems or the total managerial strategy. There may be tactical efforts which work with subparts of the organization but the "system" to be changed is a total, relatively autonomous organization. This is not necessarily a total corporation, or an entire government, but refers to a system which is relatively free to determine its own plans and future within very *general* constraints from the environment.

3. *It is managed from the top.*

In an organization-development effort, the top management of the system has a personal investment in the program and its outcomes. They actively participate in the *management* of the effort. This does not mean they must participate in the same *activities* as others, but it does mean that they must have both knowledge and *commitment* to the goals of the program and must actively support the methods used to achieve the goals.

4. It is designed to *increase organization effectiveness* and *health.*

To understand the goals of organization development, it is necessary to have some picture of what an "ideal" effective, healthy organization would look like. What would be its characteristics? Numbers of writers and practitioners in the field have proposed definitions which, although they differ in detail, indicate a strong consensus of what a healthy operating organization is. Let me start with my own definition. An effective organization is one in which:

a) The total organization, the significant subparts, and individuals, manage their work against *goals* and *plans* for achievement of these goals.

b) Form follows function (the problem, or task, or project, determines how the human resources are organized).

c) Decisions are made by and near the sources of information regardless of where these sources are located on the organization chart.

d) The reward system is such that managers and supervisors are rewarded (and punished) comparably for:
    short-term profit or production performance,
    growth and development of their subordinates,
    creating a viable working group.

e)   Communication laterally and vertically is *relatively* undistorted. People are generally open and confronting. They share all the relevant facts including feelings.

f)   There is a minimum amount of inappropriate win/lose activities between individuals and groups. Constant effort exists at all levels to treat conflict and conflict-situations as *problems* subject to problem-solving methods.

g)   There is high "conflict" (clash of ideas) about tasks and projects, and relatively little energy spent in clashing over *interpersonal* difficulties because they have been generally worked through.

h)   The organization and its parts see themselves as interacting with each other *and* with a *larger* environment. The organization is an "open system."

i)   There is a shared value, and management strategy to support it, of trying to help each person (or unit) in the organization maintain his (or its) integrity and uniqueness in an interdependent environment.

j)   The organization and its members operate in an "action-research" way. General practice is to build in *feedback mechanisms* so that individuals and groups can learn from their own experience.

Another definition is found in John Gardner's set of rules for an effective organization. He describes an effective organization as one which is *self-renewing* and then lists the rules:

The *first rule* is that the organization must have an effective program for the recruitment and development of talent.

The *second rule* for the organization capable of continuous renewal is that it must be a hospitable environment for the individual.

The *third rule* is that the organization must have built-in provisions for self-criticism.

The *fourth rule* is that there must be fluidity in the internal structure.

The *fifth rule* is that the organization must have some means of combating the process by which men become prisoners of their procedures.[1]

1   Gardner, J. W. "How to Prevent Organizational Dry Rot," *Harper's,* October 1965.

Edgar Schein defines organization effectiveness in relation to what he calls "the adaptive coping cycle," that is, an organization that can effectively adapt and cope with the changes in its environment. Specifically, he says:

> The sequence of activities or processes which begins with some change in the internal or external environment and ends with a more adaptive, dynamic equilibrium for dealing with the change, is the organization's "adaptive coping cycle." If we identify the various stages or processes of this cycle, we shall also be able to identify the points where organizations typically may fail to cope adequately and where, therefore, consultants and researchers have been able in a variety of ways to help increase organization effectiveness.[2]

The organization conditions necessary for effective coping, according to Schein, are:

—The ability to take in and communicate information reliably and validly.

—Internal flexibility and creativity to make the changes which are demanded by the information obtained (including structural flexibility).

—Integration and commitment to the goals of the organization from which comes the willingness to change.

—An internal climate of support and freedom from threat, since being threatened undermines good communication, reduces flexibility, and stimulates self-protection rather than concern for the total system.

Miles *et al.* (1966) define the healthy organization in three broad areas—those concerned with task accomplishment, those concerned with internal integration, and those involving mutual adaptation of the organization and its environment. The following dimensional conditions are listed for each area:

> In the task-accomplishment area, a healthy organization would be one with (1) reasonably clear, accepted, achievable and appropriate goals; (2) relatively understood communications flow; (3) optimal power equalization.

> In the area of internal integration, a healthy organization would be one with (4) resource utilization and individuals' *good fit* between

2   Schein, E. H. *Organizational Psychology.* Englewood Cliffs, N.J.: Prentice-Hall, 1965.

personal disposition and role demands; (5) a reasonable degree of cohesiveness and "organization identity," clear and attractive enough so that persons feel actively connected to it; (6) high morale. In order to have growth and active changefulness, a healthy organization would be one with innovativeness, autonomy, adaptation, and problem-solving adequacy.[3]

Lou Morse, in his recent thesis on organization development, writes that:

The commonality of goals are cooperative group relations, consensus, integration, and commitment to the goals of the organization (task accomplishment), creativity, authentic behavior, freedom from threat, full utilization of a person's capabilities, and organizational flexibility.[4]

5. Organization development achieves its goals through *planned interventions* using behavioral-science knowledge.

A strategy is developed of intervening or moving into the existing organization and helping it, in effect, "stop the music," examine its present ways of work, norms, and values, and look at alternative ways of working, or relating, or rewarding. In *Chapter 3* a number of types of interventions are detailed, and in *Chapters 4* through *8*, a series of cases are examined which will illustrate different types of interventions and their effects. The interventions used draw on the knowledge and technology of the behavioral sciences about such processes as individual motivation, power, communications, perception, cultural norms, problem-solving, goal-setting, interpersonal relationships, intergroup relationships, and conflict management.

Some Operational Goals in an Organization-Development Effort

To move toward the kind of organization conditions described in the above definitions, OD efforts usually have some of the following operational goals:

1. To develop a self-renewing, *viable* system that can organize in a variety of ways depending on tasks. This means systematic efforts to

3   Miles, M. B., *et al.* "Data Feedback and Organization Change in a School System," paper given at a meeting of the American Sociological Association, August 27, 1966.
4   Morse, L. H. "Task-Centered Organization Development," Master's Thesis, Sloan School of Management, M.I.T., June 1968.

change and loosen up the way the organization operates, so that it organizes differently depending on the nature of the task. There is movement toward a concept of "form follows function," rather than that *tasks* must *fit* into existing structures.

2. To optimize the effectiveness of both the stable (the basic organization chart) and the temporary systems (the many projects, committees, etc., through which much of the organization's work is accomplished) by built-in, *continuous improvement* mechanisms. This means the introduction of procedures for analyzing work tasks and resource distribution, and for building in continuous "feedback" regarding the way a system or subsystem is operating.

3. To move toward *high collaboration* and *low competition* between interdependent units. One of the major obstacles to effective organizations is the amount of dysfunctional energy spent in inappropriate competition—energy that is not, therefore, available for the accomplishment of tasks. If all of the energy that is used by, let's say, manufacturing people disliking or wanting to "get those sales people," or vice versa, were available to improve organization output, productivity would increase tremendously.

4. To create conditions where conflict is brought out and managed. One of the fundamental problems in unhealthy (or less than healthy) organizations is the amount of energy that is dysfunctionally used trying to work around, or avoid, or cover up, conflicts which are inevitable in a complex organization. The goal is to move the organization towards seeing conflict as an inevitable condition and as problems that need to be *worked* before adequate decisions can be made.

5. To reach the point where decisions are made on the basis of information source rather than organizational role. This means the need to move toward a *norm* of the *authority of knowledge* as well as the authority of role. It does not only mean that decisions should be moved down in the organization; it means that the organization manager should determine which is the best source of information (or combination of sources of information) to work a particular problem, and it is there that the decision-making should be located.

Some Characteristics of Organization-Development Efforts

Most successful organization-development efforts have the following characteristics:

1. There is a *planned* program involving the whole system.

2. The *top* of the organization is *aware of* and *committed to* the program and to the management of it. (This does not necessarily mean that they participate exactly the same way as other levels of the organization do, but that they *accept the responsibility* for the management.)

3. It is related to the *organization's mission.* (The organization development effort is not a program to improve effectiveness in the abstract. Rather it is an effort to improve effectiveness aimed specifically at creating organization conditions that will improve the organization's ability to achieve its mission goals.)

4. It is a *long-term* effort.

In my own experience, usually at least two or three years are required for any large organization change to take effect and be maintained. This is one of the major problems in organization-development efforts, because most reward systems are based on rewarding the achievement of short-term "profit" objectives. Most organization leaders are impatient with improvement efforts which take extended time. Yet, if real change is to occur and be maintained, there must be a commitment to an extended time, and a willingness to *reward* for the *process* of movement toward goals, as well as toward the specific achievement of short-term goals.

5. Activities are *action-oriented.*

(The types of interventions and activities in which organization members participate are aimed at changing something *after* the activity.)

In this respect, OD activities are different from many other training efforts where the activity itself, such as a training course or a management workshop, is designed to produce increased knowledge, skill, or understanding, which the individual is then supposed to transfer to the operating situation. In OD efforts, the group builds in connections and follow-up activities that are aimed toward *action programs.*

6. It focuses on *changing attitudes and/or behavior.* (Although processes, procedures, ways of work, etc., do undergo change in organization-development programs, the major target of change is the attitude, behavior, and performance of people in the organization.)

7. It usually relies on some form of *experienced-based learning* activities.

The reason for this is that, if a goal is to change attitudes and/or behavior, a particular type of learning situation is required for such change to occur. One does not learn to play golf or drive a car by getting increased knowledge about how to play golf or drive a car. Nor can one change one's managerial style or strategy through receiving input of new knowledge alone. It is necessary to examine present behavior, experiment with alternatives, and begin to practice modified ways, if change is to occur.

8. OD efforts work *primarily with groups.*

An underlying assumption is that groups and teams are the basic units of organization to be changed or modified as one moves toward organization health and effectiveness. Individual learning and personal change do occur in OD programs but as a fallout—these are not the *primary* goals or intentions.

Kinds of Organization Conditions that Call for OD Efforts

An essential condition of any effective change program is that somebody in a *strategic position* really *feels the need* for change. In other words somebody or something is "hurting." To be sure, some change efforts that introduce new technologies do not fit this generalization. As a general rule, if a change in people and the way they work together is contemplated, there must be a *felt need* at some strategic part of the organization. Let me list a few of the kinds of conditions or felt needs that have supplied the impetus for organization-development programs.

1. The need to change a *managerial strategy.*

As discussed in *Chapter 1,* it is a fact that many managers of small and large enterprises are today re-examining the basic strategies by which the organization is operating. They are attempting to modify their total managerial strategy including the communications patterns, location of decision-making, the reward system, etc.

2. The need to make the organization *climate more consistent* with both individual needs and the changing needs of the environment.

If a top manager, or strategically placed staff person, or enough people in the middle of the hierarchy, really feel this need, the organization is in a "ready state" for some planned-change effort to meet it.

3. The need to *change "cultural" norms.*

More and more managers are learning that they are really managing a "culture" with its own values, ground rules, norms, and power structure. If there is a felt need that the culture needs to be changed, in order to be more consistent with competitive demands or the environment, this is another condition where an organization development program is appropriate. For example, a large and successful food company, owned by two families, had operated very successfully for fifty years. All positions above the upper middle of the structure were restricted to members of the family; all stock was owned by the family; and all policy decisions were made by a family board. Some of the more progressive members of the family became concerned about the state of the enterprise in these changing times. They strongly felt the need for changing from a family-owned, family-controlled organization to a family-controlled, professionally-managed organization. The problem to be dealt with, then, was a *total change* in the *culture* of the organization, designed to arrive at different norms, different ground rules, and so forth.

This required major, long-term change-effort with a variety of strategies and interventions, in order for people to accept the new set of conditions. This was particularly true for those who had grown up within the other set of conditions.

4. The need to change *structure* and *roles.*

An awareness by key management that "we're just not properly organized," that the work of (let's say) the research department and the work of the development department should be separated or should be integrated; that the management-services function and the personnel function should report to the same vice-president; or that the field managers should take over some of the activities of the headquarters staff, etc. The *felt* need here and the problems anticipated in effecting a major structural or role change may lead to an organizational-development effort.

5. The need to improve *intergroup collaboration*.

As I mentioned earlier, one of the major expenditures of dysfunctional energy in organizations is the large amount of inappropriate competition between groups. When this becomes noticeable and top managers are "hurting," they are ready to initiate efforts to develop a program for increasing intergroup collaboration.

6. The need to *open* up the *communications system*.

When managers become aware of significant gaps in communication up or down, or of a lack of adequate information for making decisions, they may *feel* the need for action to improve the situation. Numbers of studies show that this is a central problem in much of organization life. Blake and Mouton in their Grid OD book[5] report studies of several hundred executives in which the number one barrier to corporate excellence is communications problems, in terms not only of the communication structure, but also of the *quality* of the communication.

7. The need for *better planning*.

One of the major corollaries of the increasing complexity of business and the changing demands of the environment is that the planning function, which used to be highly centralized in the president's or national director's office, now must be done by a number of people throughout the organization. Most people who are in roles requiring this skill have little formal training in it. Therefore, their planning practices are frequently crude, unsophisticated, and not too effective. An awareness of this condition by management may well lead to an organization-wide effort to improve planning and goal-setting.

8. The need for coping with *problems of merger*.

In today's world, it is more and more common for companies to merge, for divisions of organizations to merge, for church organizations to merge, for subgroups doing similar tasks to merge. In every merger situation, there is the surviving partner and the merged partner. The

5   Blake, R. R., and J. S. Mouton. *Corporate Excellence through Grid Organization Development*. Houston: Gulf Publishing Co., 1968.

human problems concerned with such a process are tremendous and may be very destructive to organization health. Awareness of this, and/or a feeling of hurting as the results of a recent merger, may well cause a management to induce a planned program for coping with the problem.

9. Need for *change in motivation* of the *work force.*

This could be an "umbrella" statement, but here it specifically refers to situations which are becoming more and more frequent where there is a need for changing the "psychological ownership" condition within the work force. For example, in some large companies there are planned efforts under way to change the way work is organized and the way jobs are defined. Herzberg's work[6] on "job enlargement" and "job enrichment" and the application of this in many organizations is evidence of the need. The Scanlon plans,[7] a shared-reward system, are examples of specific, company-wide efforts to change the motivations of a work force.

10. Need for *adaptation* to a *new environment.*

If a company moves into a new type of product due to a merger or an acquisition, it may have to develop an entirely different marketing strategy. If a company which has been production-oriented becomes highly research-oriented, the entire organization has to adapt to new role relationships and new power relationships. In one advertising agency the historic pattern was that the account executives were the key people with whom the clients did all their business. Recently, due to the advent of television and other media, the clients want to talk directly to the television specialist, or the media specialist, and have less need to talk with the account executive. The environment of the agency, in relation to its clients, is dramatically different. This has produced some real trauma in the agency as influence patterns have changed. It has been necessary to develop an organization-wide effort to examine the changed environment, assess its consequences, and determine ways of coping with the new conditions.

6   Herzberg, F., *et al. The Motivation to Work.* New York: John Wiley & Sons, 1959.
7   Lesieur, F. *The Scanlon Plan: A Frontier in Labor-Management Cooperation.* New York: The Technology Press, 1958.

THE RELATIONSHIP OF OD CHANGE EFFORTS
TO OTHER TYPES OF CHANGE EFFORTS

Since the phrase "organization development" became part of the jargon and then part of the literature of management, there have been all sorts of definitions as to its boundaries and its unique qualities. Today, organization-development practitioners represent a wide variety of backgrounds. They would also propose a wide variety of definitions as to the nature of the organization-development job. There has emerged a role in organizations which can be generically defined as a *change agent* or agent of change. This will be discussed more fully in later chapters. In brief, the primary responsibility of this role is to facilitate the improvement of organization effectiveness and health through providing interventions, development activities, and programs for organization improvement.

People performing such a role, by and large, have come out of the training business, or have been heading management-development efforts in their organizations. Their orientation is primarily toward the use of behavioral-science knowledge in the solution of these organization problems.

In order to try to clarify the *unique* characteristics of organization development, it will be necessary to examine the differences between organization-development change-efforts and other efforts which are directed toward changing human behavior or work methods.

Organization Development and Management Development

The difference between these two types of efforts is primarily in who is the customer. Management development might be more appropriately called "manager development." Its purposes usually are to upgrade the skills, abilities, and capacities of managers to handle broader assignments; to be able to move toward realizing the organization's needs for succession, promotion, and so forth. Management development includes career planning, job rotation, management education in and out of the organization, appraisal and review, etc. In all these, the target is the development, improvement, or assessment of the individual manager. *Organization development*, on the other hand, although it certainly includes management-development efforts, is primarily focused on *improving the systems* that make up the total organization. The OD effort will be primarily concerned with training *of groups,* not necessarily *in* groups;

with working on *intergroup relationships;* with examination of *communications systems* or the organization *structure* and *roles;* and with improving the goal-setting process. An example of an organization-development program activity would be a periodic assessment (as a standard practice) of how a team or family group (boss and subordinates) is operating. They set goals on a regular basis for improvement of their internal working relationships, of the way they solve problems, and of the quality of their communication, as well as establishing priorities on their future tasks. Incidentally, the individual members of such a team often learn a great deal about their own personal functioning, their interpersonal relationships, their decision-making abilities, etc., but the primary focus is the *team.*

More and more people are moving from management-development roles into organization-development positions. This frequently means developing new role relationships with the top of the organization, new skills in organization diagnosis, and new relationships with other change-efforts such as operations research and management services.

Organization Development and Training

Managements have, from time to time, seen a need for some kind of company-wide, overall training effort to upgrade the managerial effectiveness of all managers or the problem-solving of all work units. Some organizations send entire management groups to human-relations training laboratories or business-school programs. These practices would be described by many people as organization-development efforts. The difference between these and a genuine OD effort, in my opinion, is that they are not specifically related to the organization's mission; they are not *action-oriented* in the sense of providing a connecting link between the training activity and the action planning which follows it. They are not organically part of a larger effort.

This is not to say that such training efforts are not very useful, but it is to say that they do not necessarily produce *organization* change. This can be illustrated by another reference to the Blake-Mouton organization-development program. The first phase of their six-phase program is an educational one, in which participants attend a one-week laboratory-like educational experience designed to teach them concepts and give them insights into their own managerial style, into how teams work, into the problems of communications in organizations, into intergroup relations, and into processes of goal-setting and planning. Many companies have participated extensively in phase one of this program. They have assumed that this participation, plus the enthusiastic response to it that most people have, would therefore produce an organizational change. The evidence is clear that attendance and individual enthusiasm do not alone produce such an organizational change. Blake and Mouton are the first to say that this is the *first* phase of a six-phase program, and that its primary purpose is to furnish education, not to stimulate action. The organizational payoff does not come until the skills and abilities learned in the educational phase are applied by the work teams and by the organization management team. A thorough study of its relationship to the quality of its planning, its goal-setting, and its relationships, is required before organization change occurs. The above may illustrate the difference between a training orientation and an organization-development orientation. One may have a company-wide participation in an educational effort, but this is not the same thing as a total organization-development effort.

Organization Development and Operations Research

A third kind of relationship which should be examined is the relationship between organization-development efforts and operations-research change-efforts. Warren Bennis' paper, "Theory and Method in Applying Behavioral Science to Planned Organizational Change,"[8] is an important resource for analyzing this relationship. He makes a specific comparison between "planned change" (referred to as "organization development" in this publication) and "operations research." First he lists the following similarities:

1. Both are relatively recent developments.

2. Both are products of World War II.

3. Both OR and OD are problem-centered, as contrasted to the basic disciplines which emphasize concept or method; in other words, they are applied rather than focusing on the content itself.

4. Both OR and OD emphasize improvement and *optimization* of performance; to that extent they are *normative* in their approach to problems.

8   *J. Appl. Behav. Sci.,* 1965, 1, No. 4, 337-360.

5. Both OR and OD rely heavily on the application of empirical science as their main method of influence.

6. Both OR and OD rely on a relationship with clients based on confidence and valid communication.

7. Both OR and OD emphasize a systems approach to problems, meaning essentially an awareness of the interdependence within the internal parts of the system.

8. OR and OD appear to be most effective when working with systems which are *complex, rapidly changing,* and probably *science-based.*

Bennis then looks at some differences. The most crucial difference, he says, has to do with the identification of strategic variables, that is, those factors which appear to make a difference in the performance of the system under study. He lists a set of variables that would classify operations-research problems. They include inventory, allocation, queuing, sequencing, routing, replacement, competition, and search. A similar inventory of problems in the organization-development field would probably include identification of appropriate mission and values, human collaboration and conflict, control and leadership, coping with and resisting change, utilization of human resources, communication between hierarchical ranks, growth patterns, management and career development.

In other words, OR practitioners tend to select economic or engineering variables, certainly variables which are quantitative and measurable and which appear to be linked directly to the profit and efficiency of the system. The OD practitioner tends to be more concerned with the human variables and values.

Ackoff and Rivett, in the introductory chapter of their book,[9] report a case where OR was called on to help a major commercial airline decide how often it should run a class for stewardesses and how large it should be. This study involved an analysis of the following factors: cost of running the school, forecast for future requirements, forecasting procedures, expenses and salaries of all personnel, maximum possible average number of flying hours per stewardess that could be obtained, factors in stewardesses' job satisfaction, the number of reserve stewardesses required at each air base, the number of bases and where they should be located,

9   Ackoff, R. L., and P. Rivett. *A Manager's Guide to Operations Research.* New York and London: John Wiley & Sons, 1963.

how flights should be assigned, etc. As Ackoff and Rivett conclude:

> What originally appeared to be a simple and isolated problem turned out to be interconnected with almost all other operating problems of the airline. With extension of the problem, the solutions to the parts could be interrelated to assure best overall performance. This avoided a "local" improvement which might result in an overall loss of efficiency.

Bennis goes on to compare this case with a report[10] from C. Sofer, a sociologist and OD consultant.

> A small firm called on him to help in the selection of a senior manager. This "presenting symptom" led to a series of disclosures and causal mechanisms which Sofer uncovered during a series of talks and meetings with the top management group. The case itself unraveled a complicated cat's-cradle of factors including family relationships (among the top management group), fantasies and mistrust among members of the management group, management- and career-development selection procedures, etc. Sofer helped the firm overcome these problems through counseling, through devising new organization structures, through a training program, and through developing improved selection devices. The case was completed in about three visits with follow-up consultation from time to time.

The similarities and differences between organization development and operations research indicate a great need for *connection* between these two types of efforts. It should be clear that in the first case, the OR situation, there are all sorts of human factors involved which, had they also been taken into account, could have ensured a more lasting and more effective change. In the second case, there was little examination of the engineering variables, the numbers of people in the quantitative manpower planning, and so forth; such an examination might have made the efforts of Sofer and his colleagues even more effective there.

It is essential for the organization-development and the operations-research efforts to be coordinated very closely at the operating level and not just brought together in the president's office. There is a trend (and it will grow) toward more and more efforts to integrate or to coordinate and connect these efforts in the years ahead.

10   Bennis, W. "Theory and Practice in Planned Change," working paper, Sloan School of Management, M.I.T., 1965.

SUMMARY

The basic points covered here are that organization development is based on behavioral-science knowledge, it is managed from the top, and it is organization-wide in its approach. It is concerned with the development, change, and improvement of systems and subsystems. It is focused on and closely related to short- and medium-term organization mission goals; its aim is to increase organization health and effectiveness. It differs from, but may encompass, management development and training; it differs from, yet should be coordinated with, quantitative planned-change efforts such as operations research.

The next chapter will move from the general characteristics to further examination of the specific elements and types of interventions in organization-development programs.

3

STRATEGIES, TACTICS, AND ACTIVITIES
IN ORGANIZATION DEVELOPMENT

The development of a strategy for systematic improvement of an organization demands an examination of the present state of things. Such an analysis usually looks at two broad areas. One is a diagnosis of the various *subsystems* that make up the total organization system. These subsystems may be natural "teams" such as top management, the production department, or a research group; or they may be levels such as top management, middle management, or the work force.

The second area of diagnosis is the organization *processes* that are occurring. These include decision-making processes, communications patterns and styles, relationships between interfacing groups, the management of conflict, the setting of goals, and planning methods.

Several assumptions about the nature and functioning of organizations become relevant in such an analysis. The following is a partial list.

1. The basic building blocks of an organization are groups (teams). Therefore, the basic units of change are groups, not individuals.

2. An always relevant change goal is the reduction of inappropriate competition between parts of the organization and the development of a more collaborative condition.

3. Decision-making in a healthy organization is located where the information sources are, rather than in a particular role or level of hierarchy.

4. Organizations, subunits of organizations, and individuals continuously manage their affairs against goals. Controls are interim measurements, not the basis of managerial strategy.

5. One goal of a healthy organization is to develop generally open communication, mutual trust, and confidence between and across levels.

6. "People support what they help create." People affected by a change must be allowed active participation and a sense of ownership in the planning and conduct of the change.

From a diagnosis of these systems and processes, and based on the assumptions mentioned, a strategy for change emerges. It will probably include the following types of "interventions" into the organization systems and processes:

1. Working with teams on team development.

2. Working on intergroup relationships between subsystems.

3. Working on planning and goal setting processes for individuals, teams, and larger systems.

4. Working on educational activities for upgrading the knowledge, skills, and abilities of key personnel at all levels.

An examination of these categories of "interventions" and some of the tactics that are used in carrying out these strategies follow.

TEAM DEVELOPMENT

As stated above, a fundamental assumption is that the organization, as it does its work, does it through a number of work teams of different kinds. The teams may be "family" groups, that is, boss and subordinates. They may be colleague or peer groups, such as all the regional sales managers or all the division directors of an agency. They may be technical teams, such as the total personnel function or the quality-control function. They may be project teams, with members from a variety of functions brought together for some specific activity. They may be start-up teams in new enterprises. They may be the top management or the board of directors.

Almost all organization-wide planned-change efforts have, as one of their early targets of change, the improvement of team effectiveness. There are a number of types of activities used for helping teams do this.

Some of these are focused on the *"processes"* of the team, such as the development of the team's working relationships or the team's problem-solving skills. Some are focused on the *tasks* of the team, and have an action-planning or goal-setting emphasis. Regardless of the specific focus on task or relationships, there is usually a spill-over into the other area. A team-building activity explicitly designed to plan the team's work efforts in the subsequent year will probably also pay attention to the processes of the group and to the relationships of its members. If an activity is designed to focus on the relationships of the people in a group, it probably will also look at the group's goals and plans for work.

Team-building activities usually use an action-research model of intervention. There are three processes involved in the activity: collection of information; feedback of the information to the team; action planning from the feedback. These processes take different forms in different situations, but are a common characteristic of most team-building activities whether focused on relationships or work tasks.

Team-improvement activities frequently take place in a setting removed from the work place, in order that the members of the team can be away from day-to-day pressures. This type of work requires a different pace and emphasis than that required in the normal operation of the team.

There is also a learning component in the activity. Members of the team are interested in and, in some degree, committed to, learning while they work. The learning may be addressed to working better together, or setting better goals. Whatever the objective, the members of the team see, as a relevant output, that the team learns to function more effectively and, incidentally, that members learn how to function more effectively with their personal styles.

New Teams

There are a variety of situations where a new team is being formed. It may be that a new organization unit is being developed; or that a project team is being created; or that a temporary system or task force has been put together; or there has been a change in the leadership of a team. Whatever the reason for being formed, new teams have these characteristics:

1. There is a fair degree of confusion as to roles and relationships.

2. There is usually fairly clear understanding of short-term goals.

3. People who make up a new team usually have technical competence which puts them on the team, and there is a challenge in the project which will draw on their technical capacities.

4. Team leaders usually do not pay much early attention to the relationships among the new team members, because their attention is on the tasks of the team.

Experience in a variety of settings indicates that, while the early activities are focused on task and work problems, relationship problems do develop as they do in any human system. By the time these issues surface, the team may be well along in its work activities; as a result, the difficulties of working out the relationships and team processes become very costly.

It has been found that there is considerable payoff if a new team can take a short period of time at the beginning of its life to examine *collaboratively* how it is going to work together, what its methods, procedures, and work relationships will be, and what the priority concerns of its members are. Then the team works more effectively, has fewer interpersonal problems, is more productive, and is more meaningful to its members.

We shall now discuss one model that has been effective in a number of new team-development efforts. The activity usually is a one- or two-day team meeting away from the work site. It is scheduled during the first few weeks of the team's life. The specific form of the meeting varies but basically the following components are included:

1. A statement, discussion, and clarification of the mission of the group—its goals, timetable, work tasks.

2. A discussion of the concerns and hopes of the group members for this joint effort. New members of new groups frequently have concern about their roles, their relationships to the leadership, how this group will stay with or depart from tradition, the reward system, and what will happen to them when the group task is ended. An early clarification of these matters can make a significant difference.

3. A presentation and explanation of the group leader's plan to organize the work—the organization structure, relationships to other parts of the system, and general ground rules.

4. A sharing and discussion of major areas of responsibility and authority of each member. An effective procedure is one in which each

person describes what he sees as his function and responsibilities, and then checks his perceptions with the leader's perceptions and expectations, and also with those of other team members whose functions interface with his own.

5. The development of mechanisms for communications within the team such as staff meetings, memoranda, task forces, subprojects, etc. In this process, the team leader might state his preference and past experience, and check these against the preferences and past experiences of the members. A decision made at this point, with group concurrence and commitment, helps assure everyone's support to carry out the decision and make the mechanisms work. This is also a good time for the team leader to share information on his personal administrative style and practices.

6. Where appropriate, planning for the training and induction of the rest of the organization. For example, frequently, in new organizations, the *orientation* of new members of the various departments is handled independently of other departments. This causes much overlap and a lot of extra work for the top management. Attention to an integrated induction and orientation effort early in the group's life has high payoff.

7 Arrangements for a follow-up meeting. This is an important next step, particularly if the group is to continue working over an extended period of time.[1]

In a case where the new team is new because of a change in leadership, the new leader should assign priority on the agenda to a definition of his expectations, style, goals, and aspirations, and to a request for information back from the members how these fit *their* expectations and aspirations. From this information-sharing, the team can jointly establish at least short-term operating objectives and mechanisms. Collaborative goal-setting efforts at the beginning of the new leader's term significantly reduce the loss of productivity that usually follows a change of leadership.

---

1   More detail may be found in "An Action-Research Approach to Organization Improvement," paper delivered by R. Beckhard at the American Management Association Annual Personnel Conference, February 7, 1967, New York City.

Family Teams or Work Teams

Let me describe three models that have proved successful for working with such teams.

The first type uses the interview, feedback, and action-planning process mentioned earlier. In this form, a consultant (or resource outside the actual team) interviews members of the team a day or so before the team meeting. He asks each member, in a brief interview, to respond to the questions "What can be done to increase the effectiveness of the operations of this team, and of the organization? What are the obstacles to achieving this?"

The results of these interviews are tabulated and categorized under headings provided by the outside resource. The team then meets, frequently in an off-site location. The meeting begins with the resource person feeding back the information he collected from the team members. After hearing it, the first task of the group is to go through the data and set priorities. They build an agenda for working the information.

The major activity in such a meeting is the working through of the data. The group solves those problems that can be fully dealt with at the meeting. It makes action plans for dealing with those items which need to be handled by the team or some subpart of it after the meeting. It develops mechanisms for handling items that have to be forwarded on to some other part of the organization.

The focus of the entire meeting is on action-planning based on the information produced. At the end of the meeting the team usually has a list of follow-up activities, including meetings and a timetable of actions.

This form of development activity may be used to focus on improving the work of the team, on setting goals, on improving the relationships of the team members, or on all three. It is determined in large part by the nature of the problems brought up during the interviews and in the purposes of the meeting as stated by the team leader.

Another form of team building is illustrated by Blake and Mouton in their Six-Phase Organization-Development program described in their book *Corporate Excellence through Grid Organization Development* and in their sister book in this series, *How to Build a Dynamic Corporation through Grid Organization Development*. In this model, a work team attends an educational program where its members learn concepts and practice the use of various instruments to help them analyze their own team effectiveness and managerial styles. They also practice organization diagnosis and goal-setting. Following this educational phase, the team meets in another activity to look at and plan improvement of their own team effectiveness, the individual styles of their members, and the effects of these on the team's functioning; to analyze the team's relationships with other groups with which it interfaces, and diagnose the current state of the organization; and, through examination of the goal ("desired state") for the organization, to identify the gaps between the present state and the desired state.

The team employs instruments which they learned to use in the educational part of the program, and applies these to their own functioning. The program has an action orientation but within the constraints defined by the program itself and the instruments. It focuses heavily on the processes necessary to build an effective functioning team, and, if followed conscientiously, can be a most effective development activity.

A third model is one which utilizes the concept of the unstructured group. A team will go off-site for two or three days for a workshop or "laboratory." It is frequently called a laboratory because it uses the laboratory method of learning—producing behavior in the meeting, examining it, generalizing from it, and trying to apply it to the actual work setting. This model focuses more heavily on interpersonal relationships and some of the team processes such as decision-making, communications, etc. It gives secondary emphasis to action-planning and connecting the relationships to tasks, assuming that these will be done in other settings.

Functional Teams

One other form of team building activity occurring frequently in large organizations is the functional team meeting. In this activity, people performing a similar function in different locations come together periodically to exchange information and ideas, to develop standards, and to develop stronger membership in their own professional category. Such programs exist where organization leadership takes serious account of the importance of professional membership to ever-increasing numbers of people in organizations today. The format of such activities is similar to the models described, usually focusing on some sort of information collection prior to the meeting, and with an agenda-planning or priority-setting activity using this information, and some sort of action plans for the team itself and the team in relation to other parts of the organization.

Another form of pre-meeting information collecting which is sometimes used in functional team meetings (and can also be used in work or family teams) is to have each member answer questions in a letter addressed to the outside resource. Usually anonymous, these letters give the respondents' thoughts on what can be done to improve the effectiveness of the organization; what the obstacles to achievement are, and what should be priority items for inclusion on the agenda. The material is put together as it would be from the interviews and becomes the basis for the agenda.

INTERGROUP RELATIONSHIPS

I have mentioned several times that one of the major problems affecting organization effectiveness is the amount of dysfunctional energy expended in inappropriate competition and fighting between groups that should be collaborating. By the nature of organizations, there are bound to be conditions where if one department achieves its goals, it frustrates the achievement of some other group's goals. Competition for rare resources is a continuing condition and one which must be constantly managed. If the reward system in an organization is such that it requires people to meet their goals, but sets conditions over which they have no control and then punishes them for not meeting their goals, the system tends to produce frustration and a great deal of negative energy. Unfortunately, this is a rather common organization condition. Frequently, where this condition exists, the frustration takes the form of negative stereotypes of one group or another. When these stereotypes form, communication between the groups tends to decrease. Attempts to collaborate are minimal and the "game" frequently becomes one of "getting the other guy" or avoiding being "gotten" by him. Such a condition tends to perpetuate itself unless some intervention is made to try to change the win/lose, competitive condition to a win/win, problem-solving condition.

As an illustration, Department A, the production department, is required to meet a production budget. The policy of the company is that the production department should produce whatever the sales department can sell. The sales department gets a tremendous order which involves large amounts of overtime on production. This creates new problems and puts very heavy pressure on production people. This pressure produces extra tension in the production department. If the department is not rewarded for its extra effort but, as is sometimes the case, is punished for not meeting its cost budget, frustration ensues and the production group is likely to blame Sales for this condition. If the condition is a frequent one, the blame is likely to take the form of "Those sales guys don't have any understanding of the problem," or "Those sales types are on incentive and they don't care whether the organization operates effectively or not." From such stereotyping, there tends to be a "We'll show them" or "We'll ignore them" attitude. This condition is likely to remain rather stable and negative unless something specific is done about it.

There have been developed a number of specific activities to deal with such a problem. It has been found that in the space of a half-day or so, leaders and/or members of groups in such a condition can be brought together, can reduce misunderstanding, and can set up mechanisms for joint collaboration which will make a significant difference in the effectiveness of a whole organization. Here is a description of such an activity.

First, the leadership or membership of the two groups are brought together. They are asked to concur that it would be desirable as a common purpose to reduce some of the tension and frustration that exists and to see if there are ways of finding mechanisms for getting more production and more collaboration through joint effort and understanding. This is the only requirement for commitment at the beginning of the meeting.

The two groups are then sent to separate locations and asked to think about and develop a list which defines their attitudes about the other group—what it is about the other group's functioning and activities that exasperates them or gives them trouble. They are not to try for consensus, but just note their feelings and attitudes about the other group.

A second task is to develop another list of their speculations about what the other group is writing about them right now. Then the two groups are brought together—Group A reports its attitudes and feelings toward Group B, and Group B does the same with Group A. There is no discussion between the groups. Group A then reports its list of what it *thought* Group B would write about them, and Group B does the same about Group A.

The groups return to their separate locations to react to this shared information and to produce a list of issues which should have the priority attention of both groups. During this second team meeting, most teams find that a number of the issues on their first list were misunderstandings which were cleared up merely by sharing the information. They are usually also able to reduce the list, from the large number of items on the first list, to the most relevant issues to be worked.

The two groups then meet and compare their lists of issues. They make one list out of these, set priorities and agenda, and go to work in much the same way as described in the previous illustrations.

It has been found repeatedly that in a relatively short period of time, an activity of this kind makes it possible for two groups in an organization to move toward considerable change in their relationship and their work effectiveness. Typically they produce an action plan which continues over time and assures reduction of the inappropriate competition.

This design, with some modifications, is used frequently to improve headquarters-field relationships. Representatives of the headquarters organization and a field organization meet to work through the areas of difference and provide mechanisms for better collaboration. There have been several successful efforts to apply similar designs in union-management relations. Blake, Shepard, and Mouton report on some of these efforts in *Managing Intergroup Conflict in Industry.*[2]

GOAL-SETTING AND PLANNING

One of the major assumptions underlying organization-development efforts and much managerial strategy today is the need to assure that organizations are managing against goals. Healthy organizations tend to have goal-setting at all levels. As a cornerstone of their practices, individuals engage in systematic performance improvement and target-setting; groups and teams periodically and systematically set work goals and plans for achieving them; the organization as a whole engages in systematic goal-setting activities.

There are a number of organization-development activities designed to facilitate an organization's moving toward goal-setting as a way of life.

Individual Goal-Setting

It is extremely important that this process start at the top of some significant part of the organization. The goal-setting process itself, for

2   Blake, R. R., H. A. Shepard, and J. S. Mouton. *Managing Intergroup Conflict in Industry.* Houston: Gulf Publishing Co., 1965.

individual performance improvement, consists mainly of a dialogue between an individual and his immediate supervisor in which they jointly plan improvement targets and review progress toward meeting them.

The process includes the following steps. First, a description of the job is developed by the man in it. This "first-draft" description is shared by the man and his supervisor and they agree on a common definition of the job with the man in it. This becomes a contract between the two. The person in the job then sets a first draft of targets based on this description. The targets describe where he'd like to be within, say, six months; what parts of his responsibility he would like to see improved or changed, what parts stabilized, what parts deleted. These targets are then reviewed with his supervisor. The two jointly develop a second draft which is the *plan* for improvement. After the six months, the man and his supervisor jointly review progress against the goals and *jointly* set new targets for the next six months.

Before such a process can be effective there must be *real* commitment by the supervisors. It is helpful to develop a means for groups to learn to use the process. For example, if a top-management team were to decide on this type of goal setting, it would be desirable to have a preparatory activity.

First, the team could hear from an outside resource the philosophy of goal-setting, the elements of the process, the difficulties in carrying it out, and the need for commitment to make it work.

Second, the team would engage in a learning activity in which they would go through the process. Each subordinate would write a job description, and would have a preliminary discussion with the boss to arrive at a second draft.

Third, the team would come together and discuss how this phase had worked—what difficulties members had in working out the descriptions; whose description was used; ways of improving the procedure.

The team would then practice the new step—setting the targets. Each man would set first-draft targets, then compare his targets with his boss. Together they would arrive at a second draft. After each subordinate and the common boss had done this, the team would meet to examine the problems in this phase. Only afterwards would they begin to initiate the process with their own subordinates and again go through this learning cycle.

This process is variously called "management by objectives," "target-setting," or "individual performance-improvement goal-setting." Target-setting programs tend to fail more often than they succeed because there is not a systemwide, planned procedure for introducing the program into the organization and getting *commitment* of all concerned, along the way.[3]

Team Goal-Setting

A number of models exist for systematic team goal-setting. One is a periodic annual or semiannual meeting of the team, preceded by individual work by the members on goals for the team and priorities as they see them. Using this information as a base, and working within organization goals, the team sets its targets and priorities for the next six months or year. It also defines specifically the role relationships and leadership of the projects necessary to achieve the goals. It looks at the relationship problems that might affect achievement of the work goals, and develops mechanisms for identifying and working on such problems.

Another form of team goal-setting is an inherent part of the Blake-Mouton Grid OD system, to which reference has been made previously. In this system, the team, using instruments, specifically plans its business objectives, team-development goals, and priorities, and defines specific responsibilities for achieving them.

Larger System or Organization-Wide Goal-Setting

One model of organization-wide activity has been used by a number of organizations. The top management of the division or organization sets corporate or divisional goals for profit, performance, sales, organization growth, manpower, etc. Each unit down to the bottom level independently sets its own goals with the knowledge of, but not the restriction to, the corporate goal at this time. These unit goals are fed to the top of the organization, which then looks at the discrepancies between the corporate goal and the sum of the unit goals. If there is a discrepancy, this is noted, and an analysis of the incompatibility is sent back to the system; all units are then asked to develop a strategy for closing the gap. From this second set of goals, the final corporate goals are formulated.

This process may sound very similar to normal business planning. However, there are several major differences. It is a truly collaborative

---

3   For further information, see *Chapter 6.* "A Critique of Performance Appraisal," in Douglas McGregor's *Human Side of Enterprise,* and his article "An Uneasy Look at Performance Appraisal," *Harv. Bus. Rev.,* **35,** No. 3, May-June 1957.

process, in which every unit of the organization has some ability to influence the final goals. It implies understanding that the relevant sources of information are located throughout the organization, and that the unit goals will influence the corporate goal. It meets the criterion of ownership by large numbers of members of the organization in the development of corporate goals, and the criterion also of getting "best" information for the top management to make its decisions. There is evidence that where there is commitment throughout the organization, the goals tend to be higher and the rate of achievement toward them also tends to be higher, than where people are asked to respond to goals set from above without having an opportunity to influence them.

Another form of organization goal-setting activity is what is called an "organization confrontation" meeting. This is usually a one-day activity which can be used to bring together a large segment of an organization in order to set priorities and action targets. The activity is particularly appropriate in situations where an organization is in stress; where, for example, there is a new top management, where there has been a loss of a major customer, or where the organization is going into a new product or a new area of business. Organizationally, this meeting is most appropriate where the top group is relatively cohesive but there is a gap between the top and the rest of the organization.

The activity is designed to mobilize the whole organization in a very short period of time toward an action plan and priorities for change and improvement. It takes the following form.[4]

Let us suppose that there are eighty people in the management from the general manager down through first-line supervision. This meeting includes all eighty members. The meeting itself takes between 4½ and 6 hours and could easily be divided into two time units—an afternoon and the following morning, or an evening and a morning. Let's assume we are using a night and a morning. The evening session has the following elements.

A general meeting includes a brief introduction by the general manager and possibly a statement by an outside resource if one is used. The statements define the purposes of the meeting, stress that this is an opportunity for everyone to influence the actions of the organization, and urge that people be open and say what they think. Assurances should be

---

4   Described in greater detail in R. Beckhard, "The Confrontation Meeting," *Harv. Bus. Rev.*, March-April 1967, 45, No. 2.

provided that no one will be punished for what they say and that anonymity will be preserved insofar as possible.

The group is divided into small groups of five or six people across organization lines, so that no boss is in the same group with a subordinate or working colleague. The top-management group, excluding the general manager, meets as one group and not with one of the heterogeneous subgroups.

The task of these groups is information collecting. The groups are assigned the following task: "Thinking of yourself as a person with needs and goals in this organization, and also thinking of the total organization, what are the behaviors, procedures, ways of work, attitudes, etc., that should be different so that life would be better around here?" Each group is asked to make a list of its items. They have about an hour for this task.

The total group then reassembles. The lists of the subgroups are placed on the board. From this total list, categories of problems are developed by the meeting leader. This marks the end of the evening meeting.

In the morning, another general session takes place. Each participant receives a copy of the information collected from the groups the night before, along with a cover page listing the category headings. The total group then participates in assigning category headings to each item on the list under the direction of the meeting leader and/or general manager.

The group then divides into functional groups under the leadership of those reporting to the general manager. For example, everyone in the manufacturing area would meet together, chaired by the head of manufacturing; the same with finance, personnel, etc. These groups would have the following tasks:

1. Go through the entire list and select three or four items which must affect you or your group. Determine what action your group will take on those and the timetable for beginning work on the problems. Be prepared to report this out to the total group.

2. Go through the list again and select those items to which you think top management should be giving highest priority. (Criteria for inclusion on this list is that your group can't deal with it.)

3. Since this is a large meeting, and all of us are off the job, develop a tactical plan for communicating what happened at this meeting to those who are not here.

The group reconvenes and each subunit reports out its list of three or four priority items and its plans for dealing with them. Then each group reports its suggestions for top management. A cumulative list of suggestions is developed. The top manager responds to this list, making some commitment on each item.

The top manager would then set a follow-up meeting for the near future, say, in five or six weeks; two hours should be allotted for such a meeting, in which the manager is committed to report progress on the items on his list and expects to receive reports of progress on other items from the various units.

The expectation of a follow-up meeting sustains "positive tension" in the system and keeps the whole organization focusing toward goals.

This model tends to produce rather dramatic organization results in a very short period of time.

EDUCATION: SKILLS AND ABILITIES
FOR INDIVIDUAL PARTICIPANTS

Although it has been said several times in this book that individual learning and the development of skill and ability are not the primary targets of an organization-development effort, they are still part of the target. There are specific skills and abilities that are more relevant than others for achieving the kind of organization effectiveness and health toward which OD efforts are aimed.

The following lists some of these and relates them to specific types of activities which are available both inside and outside organizations.

1. *Interpersonal Competence.* This includes self-awareness, communication skills, ability to manage conflict, and tolerance for ambiguity—all essential requirements for the organization leader in today's and tomorrow's world. Laboratory-training activities, sensitivity training, and Grid training, all have, as part of their purposes, this type of learning output.[5]

5   Further details on this kind of activity can be obtained from the NTL Institute for Applied Behavioral Science, Washington, D.C.

2. *Problem-Solving Knowledge and Skills.* The Kepner-Trego[6] problem-solving, decision-making clinics, and the Managerial Grid (referred to in *Chapter 1,* page 9) have this learning goal in their programs.

3. *Skills in Goal-Setting.* A number of organizations conduct clinics and provide consultation in goal-setting. Walter Mahler[7] and Malcolm Shaw[8] have developed programs for introducing and managing target-setting or "management by objectives" goal-setting, as has Urwick Orr, Limited, in England. These are specific programs which can be used inside the company for individual performance-improvement goal-setting and team goal-setting.

4. *Skills in Planning.* This is an area which has received too little attention and there are still very few formal programs available. The Blake-Mouton OD program is probably the most effective activity of this kind and I predict that major efforts will be expended in developing this area in the next few years.

5. *Understanding the Processes of Change, and Changing.* In the last two years, several educational activities have emerged which have been designed to meet this particular need. In the curricula of the business schools, such as M.I.T., Harvard, Case Western Reserve, U.C.L.A., the University of New Hampshire, and the State University of New York at Buffalo, there are specific programs moving toward the development of change technology. Several organizations conduct workshops for personnel and management and organization-development people, as well as for line people, on the process of change. The NTL Institute for Applied Behavioral Science started a program in 1967 for specialists in organization training and development which has been attended by some 75 "change agents" and managers from a variety of organizations throughout the world.

6. *Skills in System Diagnosis.* Again, there is little formal training available in this field although the above mentioned activities do have this as one of their major foci. There is a great deal of informal, intracompany

6   Kepner-Trego, Inc., Princeton, N.J.
7   Mahler Associates, Inc., Midland Park, N.J.
8   Educational Systems and Designs, Inc., Westport, Connecticut.

activity concerned with the problems of system diagnosis. More and more behavioral-science-oriented consultants are building this in as an essential part of their work. In several large industrial organizations there are informal "organizations" representing a variety of functions and levels of management who meet regularly to examine the state of the system and to look at the status of the various efforts to upgrade it. Such groups exist specifically for diagnostic reasons and wield a great deal of influence with no official authority.

SUMMARY

This chapter has looked at some of the processes and elements of organization life to which organization-development efforts are directed. It has described some of the forms of interventions or activities that are initiated to work with these elements. Lastly, it has listed some of the individual learnings, both in skills and abilities, that are prerequisites for, and receive major emphases in, such efforts.

PART 2

ORGANIZATION DEVELOPMENT STRATEGIES AT WORK

The next five chapters will examine cases of planned organization improvement. Each case illustrates a different prime change goal:

changing the organization's culture,

changing the managerial strategy,

changing the way work is done,

creative adaptation to a new environment,

changing communications and influence patterns.

4

A CASE OF CHANGING AN ORGANIZATION'S CULTURE

This case describes a strategy for changing the "culture" of an organization, in this instance, from a family-owned, *family*-managed organization to a family-owned, *professionally* managed organization.

BACKGROUND

A large food and catering company (annual sales volume $600,000,000; 30,000 employees) had, over the years, enjoyed a commanding position in its markets. In recent years this position had deteriorated seriously. Major causes for this included increased competition and increased costs, both of which had contributed to a squeeze on profits. Other causes were a rather "traditional" marketing strategy not geared to the times, and a relatively rigid management style.

The company culture was modeled on a "royalist" pattern with the family members holding all the top management jobs. (Your father had to be a member of the owning family for you to hold any job above department head.) Most of the management and work force were long-term employees and were generally satisfied with this state of affairs. There had been relatively little pressure for productivity and efficiency. Historically the organization had existed in a relatively stable, predictable world. There was a heavy production orientation in the organization so that production people had highest influence on the top management.

THE NEED

One of the more progressive and more influential members of the family (we'll call him Mr. A) headed several sections of the enterprise including the largest single business. He was acutely aware of the problems in the organization; the need for increased marketing capability; the need for new organization forms, and the need for promotion by merit rather than heredity. He and some of his brothers undertook to persuade their family colleagues to consider moving toward a change in the culture and the introduction of more professional management. After some years of negotiation, they were able to get approval for an experimental change program in the largest business segment.

At this point Mr. A called in consultants to help diagnose the situation and develop a change strategy.

INITIAL DIAGNOSIS AND STRATEGY

As the initial consultant, I worked with the family member and a member of the personnel staff. We addressed ourselves first to the following questions:

What is the specific change problem?
What systems and subsystems are specifically affected?
What is the "state" of each of these subsystems?
How *ready* for change? How *capable* to make the change?

The change problem was defined as changing the management of this division from a relatively low-autonomy group, with centralized decision-making by the family leadership, to a *relatively* autonomous profit center with professional management. A secondary change target was to continue to move the culture of the business from a heavily production-technical orientation to a more heavily marketing-oriented stance.

The systems most affected were

1. The family member who had been manager and would now be a group executive.

2. The new division manager.

3. The top division staff who now reported to a family member and would report to the new man (presently one of their colleagues).

4. Several of the corporate staff groups which interfaced with the division management and in which control was divided.

We looked at each "system's" readiness and capability for change.

	Readiness	Capability
Family member	High	High
New division manager	High	High
Top division staff	Medium to low	Low to high
Corporate functional groups	Medium to low	Medium to high

The above analysis was arrived at through discussions with key people in each of the systems. Additional facts about the state of things were:

1. There was some high management potential in the existing management team of the division.

2. The change in management would be very dramatic and probably traumatic for a number of management people.

3. The first professional manager should have a strong marketing capability.

4. There was such a man heading the marketing function in the division (Mr. B).

5. He had some relationship problems with some of his colleagues, partly due to his personal style but largely due to his role and the increased stature of marketing in the company.

6. If Mr. B were to be the "nominee," it would be necessary to give him an opportunity to further develop a *general* management orientation and to work on his own management style before the organization change.

7. It would be necessary to prepare the division-management group for the change, to get out some of their feelings and attitudes about the new leadership, and to find ways of getting their commitment to making the new mode work.

8. The family member, Mr. A, who would move out of direct management operations and function as a group executive to whom the division manager would report, was well loved and respected by the team. His personal conviction and desire to really carry out the

change would have to be well communicated to the members of the team.

9. Mr. A would have to be prepared to fully support Mr. B's decisions.

Based on this diagnosis, the following initial strategy was developed:

1. Mr. B would go to an advanced management program at a major business school.

2. An off-site meeting would be held with the top management team immediately following his return from the course and before any public announcement was made.

3. Just prior to this meeting all members of the group would be interviewed by the consultant to get their feelings and thoughts about the barriers to optimum effectiveness in the division management; the kinds of changes they would like to see occur; their concerns about a "non-family" manager; their career problems and interests.

4. The actual changeover of management would not take place for several months after the first off-site meeting.

5. Following the actual announcement, additional kinds of activities would be scheduled, including team building with the new management team, some work on intergroup relationships between the new team and the relevant central-staff services, and some goal-setting activities for the management team and later for the subunits of the division.

ACTIONS

1. Mr. B went to the business school course.

2. During the period of the course, he met several times with me. We talked about his role in the planned off-site meeting, including some of the problems that would exist with his colleagues. I made it clear that an essential condition for an effective team meeting was his *personal* conviction of the worth of such an activity, his commitment to doing it, and his willingness to openly discuss whatever information came out on business or organization problems or on attitudes and feelings of his colleagues.

Without such commitment, I proposed we should not hold the team meeting. Mr. B originally was quite skeptical about the worth of this activity. As he thought more about it, he decided that it *would* be useful to bring the group together to clear the air and begin to build toward a new team. He saw this as practical since it was similar to the way he had operated in his marketing leadership role with the marketing team.

3. During this same period (the 12-week course) Mr. B returned to his company for a meeting with Mr. A. The purpose was to think through the new role relationships between the two men and to decide how things would be handled and decisions made in this new mode.

4. After the course ended, as previously planned, I interviewed the nine members of the management group about their feelings concerning the change; about the kind of organization and the kind of management that would be required to improve the division's position in the field and to build a stronger organization. Several interesting findings emerged from these interviews.

a) Several who were interviewed felt threatened by the change. They had spent their entire working lives reporting to a "member of royalty," the *family,* and now were about to find themselves reporting to a "commoner," one of *them.* This was perceived as a loss of status, both in the firm and in the community. It was also seen as a loss of contact and upward influence with the power center, since the family would still own the business.

b) Another significant finding was the deep concern expressed by the production and technical people about the increasing influence of the marketing people. The change was perceived as a real takeover by the marketing "hot shots."

c) Some others interviewed feared they would be faced with more restrictions, and would have less autonomy and less influence.

d) There was a considerable lack of trust in the real motivations of the family in making the change. Was this a gimmick? Was it for real? What were the intentions of the family? Was this a device to upgrade marketing? What would happen to the young and sometimes incompetent family members; would they *really* be asked to report to a non-family manager?

e) A number of other historical problems surfaced in the interviews. A real conflict had existed between the technology and production departments as to who should control quality in the production process.

f) The financial manager had his primary loyalties in the central finance office, which he saw as his "home." He felt that he was a representative of the family ownership in the division. He was not a "regular" member of the management team and he did not see himself as really accountable to the general manager. He feared that Mr. B's appointment would be a threat to his role. He felt there would have to be a confrontation between the headquarters financial people and the new division manager to get things straight.

5. The day after the data were collected, Mr. A, Mr. B, the department heads, and the consultants (myself and an in-company personnel man) went away for a three-day meeting. The first evening was spent in an informal get-together by the group while the consultants were summarizing the data that had been collected. The next morning I fed back the interview results to the group. We had put the information into several categories. There was a group of items about Mr. A's intentions, motivations, reasons, and plans; a second group, related to attitudes toward Mr. B; and another group of items about the fears of a marketing takeover. A fourth group related to the financial management situation; a fifth, to intergroup or interdepartmental difficulties, including the technical/production quality-control problem. A final category dealt with division policies and practices.

After the feedback of the total information, the group selected one set of items on which they wanted to work. It quickly became apparent to all that it would be necessary to hear from Mr. A about his plans and intentions before anything else could be profitably discussed. He was quite prepared to do this. He made an open disclosure about his thinking, his feelings about the firm, about the question of promotion through competence versus heredity; about the difficulties he'd had in getting support from some of the family colleagues for his ideas; and about his strong conviction as to the necessity to continue down this course. He responded to a number of questions, including some about other younger family members, two of whom were present, and who would now move into roles subordinate to a non-family man. He announced his planned timetable for making the general announcement of the change several months after this meeting. To his surprise, the group suggested strongly that, after hearing him and seeing the situation, it made much more sense to them for him to make the change immediately. They suggested, "Let's start the new ball game and get to work on increasing the productivity and effectiveness of the organization." He agreed to this new timetable.

The next major agenda item was the feelings and anxieties about Mr. B, who was to be their boss. Using the interview information as a starting point, there was a very frank discussion of their concerns. Mr. B was queried about his past managerial style and proposed practices. People expressed their concerns about his past over-controlling style. Some voiced the worry that he would favor marketing to the detriment of other departments. He responded to these questions and shared his plans and concerns. He asked for continuing feedback on his behavior in the months ahead. He and the group worked out mechanisms for keeping this subject on the agenda for the next few months at all staff meetings.

At the end of the three days, a number of positive action steps emerged. These included:

a. Scheduling a similar off-site meeting for the technical and production managements to work through their problems of relationship and control.

b. A reorganization of the administrative staff.

c. A rethinking of the kinds of agenda to be dealt with at staff meetings.

d. An agreement to have at least one meeting a month that would look at how the management group was functioning so that continuous temperature-taking was part of the process.

e. An agreement to have this whole group function as members of the management staff for three months, but with the knowledge that it was the intention of Mr. B to cut down this very large team.

f. Recognition that it might be too difficult for some management people to accommodate to the change in management style from Mr. A's to Mr. B's style—that this would be a matter for continued discussion and negotiation.

g. An agreement to examine the financial-management role question.

h. Clarification on how Mr. A, in his new role as group executive, would participate in division matters. For example, he would no longer attend management meetings except as specifically requested.

i. An agreement on the conditions under which matters were to be brought to Mr. B or to Mr. A.

6. The next step was for an extensive team-building and goal-setting program by the top team. This went on for several months. Their

continued work together did build a cohesive and quite enthusiastic team with one exception—the financial manager. He became more and more uncomfortable and his performance more frustrating to his colleagues. A series of meetings was set up between the central financial-management staff and Mr. B., who strongly believed in decentralized control. A new arrangement was worked out which was different from the traditional patterns of highly centralized control that had existed in the company. The financial manager was transferred back to the central office. A new man was brought in from outside who had an operating orientation. He was able to provide the management with accounting and management services that Mr. B felt were essential and, at the same time, to meet the needs of the central office for financial information.

7. Moving down the organization, the members of the top team began spending so much of their time and energy with each other that they began to lose contact with the people immediately below them. The middle managers began griping to the personnel staff and to Mr. B. They felt they had less communication to and from the top than before. They felt helpless to influence the division. They felt their bosses were less accessible than in the past.

As he became aware of this, Mr. B talked with his top team, which did not see the problem as clearly as he did. Mr. B felt that immediate action was required. He asked for some consulting help. After examining the situation, we decided on a meeting of the entire management group to get the feelings aired, the priority problems identified, and action plans started for dealing with these priorities.

From this situation we invented the confrontation meeting described in *Chapter 3*. A one-day meeting was held in a hotel. After an opening session, the total management group met in small *ad hoc* groups. They identified problems and behaviors that were getting in the way of communications and performance. They then met in functional teams: sales, marketing, production, engineering, and finance. They took information from the *ad hoc* groups and made plans for doing something about it. Each group also produced a list of items to which Mr. B and the top team should give priority attention. In a general session, Mr. B responded to each of these. He made a commitment to action of some sort on each item.

This meeting tended to bring the whole organization together and to mobilize a considerable amount of energy toward systematic organization improvement. In effect, it was an organization-wide, *goal-setting* exercise.

8. Changes in an organization of this kind do not stay stable, and a few months later another off-site meeting seemed indicated. Let me quote from a talk made by Mr. B at a national management meeting some years later. His talk describes the whole effort but what follows looks specifically at this phase:

And then the top team began to get frustrated with itself, feel cynical of its own achievements—I now find I didn't believe at the time that they would be, but the top team then went through the same process of confrontation. We sat down again over two or three days with the aid of Dick Beckhard and worked through the problems, in a very candid and open way, that were bugging us. What were the barriers to team effectiveness? Now these exercises involve talking about things which might, in another culture, sound like weakness. Sometimes we lacked competence. Well, we all knew we lacked competence in a certain area. We all talked about our lack of competence in certain areas in the back staircase, but were we willing to confront it? What were the risks in so doing—would there be a blowup? Would somebody resign? Would somebody get fired? We took the risk and in fact this turned out to be a fear which was unsubstantiated. Also the question of trust—did we really trust other people? One looked at the actual behavior of members of the group and saw the way in which that behavior, predicated as it was on certain assumptions about how to be effective, did nothing but arouse anger, mistrust, and anxiety in other members of the team. We then made a conscious attempt to look at the top team to see how we could reduce these barriers. I want to emphasize my grave concern about this exercise. Was this weakness? Was I letting the lunatics run the asylum? Was I abdicating this thing called leadership? Or was this leadership? Well, it seemed to work out okay, so we then passed on to the next logical phase: It's all right for the top management—what about the operating management? So we went through the process as a division, then, of trying to get the entire management, I suppose between 150 and 250 people, to have this same kind of experience, to go through the same processes which in a more intensive way we had gone through.

9. They set up a series of programs using the managerial Grid. Their entire management-organization went to these programs. Senior division-management attended laboratory-training programs; team-development meetings were held with marketing, sales, and production groups, and systematic annual team goal-setting meetings were started.

Let me go back to another quote from Mr. B's remarks to the management association:

> What have we got from this exercise? We believe we have obtained, as a product, a freed-up society—candor is practiced—confrontation is valued—goal orientation—new patterns of behavior, sounder concepts, sounder values—task-group possibilities—maximization of resources.

He then goes on to describe a number of specific things that are different—hourly people showing considerably more concern about quality control and efficiency and effectiveness; foremen being concerned about absenteeism much more than they used to be and being concerned about job satisfaction. Another quote:

> I think we had something like fifteen committees four years ago. Apart from the top-management group who get together on Monday afternoons, I believe I'm right in saying we don't have any committees at all. This is not to say we do not have effective task groups. We have, I think, a sounder concept of the organization. I know of no organization charts in my business; I just don't find it necessary. The funny thing is the people who lived by knowing where they stood on the pyramid in relation to Fred next door or Joe in the next block no longer (it seems to me) worry about these things. I think that there are sounder values—that contribution towards running the business is now expected. Participation is your duty, not a right that is conferred on you after some years with the company.

One last quote:

> We are running a business now that's considerably bigger and more complex and more active, with something just over a third of the people we had before. We have a top team of which I am a member. We don't even call them grade-one and grade-two managers anymore. And just below that we have a team of 25 people. These men are joined in discussions with the top team about the state of the business. They're parties to our marketing analysis; they know why business is good or bad, they know what our strengths are and what our weaknesses are. The subordinates in the organization work happily not only with their own bosses but with somebody else's boss, and I think that's rather important. So at any one time, if there's a problem, the emphasis now is on problem-solving, not the preservation of hierarchy.

SUMMARY AND ANALYSIS

This case describes the first steps in an organization-wide effort to change the culture of an enterprise from family-owned, family-managed to family-owned, professionally managed.

The strategy was to start the change with a pilot effort in a significant (largest business) sector of the enterprise. The basis for this strategy choice was developed by the management with consultant help. Significant factors were:

1. The change would be dramatic and probably traumatic.

2. Many new relationships would have to be established.

3. Many would fear the change so it would need to be not too threatening.

4. The first efforts had to be successful if further efforts were to be effective.

5. The top management (family) needed to learn how to handle the change, so a pilot effort was best.

Having decided the pilot population, a diagnosis of that environment was made. Using a "model of planned change from behavioral-science research" the management and consultant developed:

1. A refinement of the statement of the change problem.

2. An analysis of the relevant units of the organization.

3. An analysis of each unit's attitudes and capacity to handle the change.

From this diagnosis, an *action strategy* was developed. It included:

1. Attitude assessment and development for top management (Mr. A).

2. Attitude change, behavior change, and wider orientation for the new division manager (Mr. B—business school, consulting conferences).

3. Attitude analysis, behavior change for division team (interviews, first off-site, follow-up meeting).

4. Change in influence of middle management (confrontation meeting).

In order to assure up to date information on the effects of the change effort, a number of information-collecting mechanisms were developed.

These included:

1. Follow-up minutes on action plans from first off-site.

2. Periodic discussion on the "state of things" between both outside and inside consultants with Mr. A, Mr. B, and top-team members.

3. Total organization confrontation meetings.

4. Periodic temperature-taking within teams (management team, functional teams, and task groups).

5. Building in critique or analysis as an organic part of staff and other meetings.

The consultant roles in this case were:

1. To help in a total-organization diagnosis and strategy plan (pilot project).

2. To provide a model for analyzing the change problem and strategy (system analysis).

3. To counsel with key individuals and pairs (Mr. A, Mr. B, production manager) on roles and relationships.

4. To get information on the state of the system and to feed it back (division team, total group, departments).

5. To function as procedural guide and consultant at team-development meetings (division team, division and group managers).

6. To convene and consult with groups having interface difficulties (production, technical).

7. To counsel with key management on continuing strategies (Mr. A, Mr. B).

8. To periodically "take a reading" with the organization on its own health and effectiveness as a basis for planning.

5

A CASE OF CHANGING THE MANAGERIAL STRATEGY

This case illustrates a strategy for change from an autocratic, centralized management style to a team-managed organization.

BACKGROUND

The organization is a small company in the materials-handling industry. There are around 500 employees. Annual sales volume during the period under discussion ranged from eight to eighteen million dollars.

The company enjoyed a good position in a highly competitive market, mainly due to its outstanding technical capability which showed in the capacity to solve customer technical problems and to maintain consistently high product quality.

The company was founded by the father of the current president. Until very recently it was a closely-held company with all of the stock in control of the family and the controlling interest in the hands of the president, whom we shall call Mr. C. Mr. C had grown up in the business and had taken over as chief executive officer about eight years prior to the change effort. His father still retained the title of chairman. The managerial strategy and style of leadership of the father was total direction and control, highly centralized decision-making. The business was a very personalized one, in relation to both employees and customers. There was heavy emphasis on high-quality products. Historically, there was limited concern for technical *innovation* as differentiated from technical quality. The company had had such innovation in its earlier years and had pioneered in a particular application of materials-handling which accounted in large part for its very good position in the market.

Modern marketing and managing methods were not of primary concern to the older, very successful, entrepreneurial chairman. His son was an entirely different type. He was concerned with an analytic approach to problems, with the application of modern management technology in all areas. When he became chief executive officer, Mr. C decided that, unlike his father who ran a one-man show, he, the son, would develop a management team using modern management methods. To help achieve this, he had steeped himself in management education, attending all sorts of courses and programs; he had hired a personnel/in- dustrial-relations man who was beginning to establish some "modern" policies and practices in the personnel area; he had brought in a new, highly efficient manufacturing manager to replace one of the older men who had grown up with the business. He was working hard to develop a smoothly functioning management team.

Unfortunately, his progress was considerably slower than his enthusiasm warranted. The historic relationships of various members of the team with the father, as well as with Mr. C, did not change significantly under the new strategy. The vice-president of engineering, one of the best technical men in the business, was seen by himself and others as not equally vulnerable to the conditions governing other key staff. He insisted, as he had in the past, on full control of the quality of the product. He personally supervised every technical activity. He was less than fully concerned about the problems of manufacturing if they interfered with his standards. The marketing man, who had grown up with Mr. C, was acutely conscious of their historical relationship. He had felt some rejection from Mr. C in recent times, particularly when Mr. C expressed dissatisfaction with the way the marketing program was being handled.

The personnel director was really trying to carry out the mandate of the president to modernize personnel policies and practices, but his method of doing this was somewhat evangelistic. Consequently he sometimes incurred resistance and downright hostility from some of his colleagues.

At about this time, Mr. C attended a management workshop for presidents. He became acquainted in some depth with the behavioral-science-oriented concepts of organization behavior, including Douglas McGregor's work and Blake and Mouton's Managerial Grid.

THE NEED

While attending this laboratory, as an exercise, he did an analysis of his own personal managerial style, and an analysis of the characteristics of his organization. These analyses both showed that for him to achieve his goals of real team management, he would need to pursue a quite different strategy including changing his managerial style and the managerial climate in his organization. In spite of his past efforts, his personal style was, in fact, management by control although his values were more toward management by participation. The styles of his immediate subordinates covered a wide range from laissez faire to highly autocratic, and the fact that he, the president, wanted a team, did not in fact change anybody else's style. The fact that he also owned the company made some of his moves toward participative management a little harder to sell.

Following the workshop he sought consultant help.

INITIAL DIAGNOSIS AND STRATEGY

The first steps in the diagnosis were to continue further the analysis of the organization's history and the current state of the relationships and managerial styles of the members of the top team.

The change "model" described in the previous chapter was applied (i.e., defining the nature of the problem; listing appropriate "systems" affected by the problem; determining each "system's" readiness and capacity to change).

The change problem was defined as moving to real action by the management team (excluding the father, who was due to retire from an active management role) in changing to a different style of managing the organization based on McGregor's Theory Y assumptions. Operationally, this would mean changing ways of operating, relocating some decision-making, establishing some interdepartmental organizations, changing authority and responsibilities.

The appropriate "systems" were identified as the president, the management team, manufacturing management, marketing management, and engineering management. The initial analysis of readiness and capability could be described thus:

	Readiness	Capability
President	High	High
Management team	Medium	High
Manufacturing management	Low to medium	Medium
Marketing management	Low	Medium to high
Engineering management	Medium	High

The initial change strategy plan was developed. Several assumptions behind the plan were:

Although there was a total organization climate-change needed, the first "organization" to change must be the top-management group.

This change would take some time. Traditions, managerial styles and relationships were firmly entrenched.

The president (Mr. C) would have to look at his own behavior, with his subordinates, and be prepared to get information on it and its effects, if open communication was to occur at the top.

The management group would have to be convinced that Mr. C really wanted this change for sound reasons, not just as a new gimmick. There was some suspicion of his previous enthusiasm for "fads."

The management group would have to demonstrate, through its own functioning, its commitment to a participative management style, as a prerequisite to much commitment to a new style down the line.

The strategy included the following activities in the early phases:

1. A team development program for the top team which would include:

    a)   An off-site meeting with some prework to analyze the team's and individuals' functioning.

    b)   Follow-up meetings at the plant if desired by the team.

2. Educational meetings between top-team members and their subordinates to explain the overall change goals.

3. Individual educational experiences for top-team members.

ACTIONS

1. *First Steps.* The president went back to his group and shared his feelings about the problem and the need for a major change. He proposed that at their annual, one-week planning conference scheduled four months from then, they take the first few days to look at (with consulting help) their own relationships, their ways of working, communications, etc. This was agreed to by all with varying degrees of enthusiasm and skepticism and with real resistance by one member.

As prework before the conference, each member of the team filled out an analysis of his own personal managerial style and key managerial orientations using the Blake-Mouton Managerial Grid. Each subordinate filled out this same information about Mr. C and he filled one out for each of them. Each of the team members also rated all his colleagues. This material was analyzed by Scientific Methods, Inc., and the analysis sent to the author who was the team consultant.

The team met at a retreat location as planned. After Mr. C again reviewed his hopes and goals for improved team effectiveness, the first activity was to develop a list of problems that were inhibiting optimum effectiveness of this team. The first day was spent working on these problems together, looking for causes, possible solutions, and next action steps. Each item was either resolved, referred to the planning conference of the following days, deferred for action in subsequent management meetings, or assigned to task forces.

On the second day, the consultant presented the analysis of each member's managerial style, starting with the president, Mr. C. The report included what the man, himself, had written, what his boss, Mr. C, had written, and what his colleagues had written.

These reports provided a useful vehicle for a fruitful discussion among the group. They uncovered a lot of blocks to effective work relationships due to stereotypes, misunderstandings, traditions, and lack of information.

A third activity was to again review barriers to team effectiveness, including individual styles, and to update the list of "next steps" made at the end of the first day.

One output of this meeting was that the group decided they would meet with the consultant to work this type of agenda at least four times during the following year. They also decided to institute a brief process "analysis" or critique at the end of each of their regular meetings, and to do the same in the immediately upcoming planning conference.

2. *Top-Team Follow Up Activities.* The group continued to work on improving their own functioning. Their effectiveness improved considerably during the following year. They were able to deal effectively with more complicated issues and their communication became more open. One problem they had during this phase was that they became so conscious of "process" and relationships that they became very "tender" with each other. The result was that some conflicts were not worked through very meaningfully.

3. *First Attempts to Move Program Down.* There were some very specific efforts by one or two members to start applying new methods to their own management. The vice-president of manufacturing started regular improvement meetings with his staff. Down the line, the production superintendent started regular improvement meetings with the foreman. Each work group in the plant became involved in monthly "operations improvement" meetings for their unit. Task forces were set up between subunits in production to iron out difficulties such as parts shortages and inspection delays. On the surface it looked as if tremendous change was occurring.

In fact, there was a lot of activity related to "operations improvement" directed from the top but no real change in managerial attitudes as seen by those in the middle.

4. *First Review.* As planned, the consultant took the "temperature" of the organization a few months after all this activity was initiated. He talked with supervisors and hourly work force to get a reading on their attitudes toward the change.

The basic attitude throughout was that top management was "trying" to get some more participative management into the organization but nothing really was changing. One middle manager who had done his homework said, "We're going Theory Y in a Theory X manner."

5. *Individual Educational Activity for Management.* At about the same time these activities were occurring, the members of the management group were attending management laboratories of various kinds. Some went to sensitivity training workshops of the NTL Institute type, and others attended Grid labs. As a result of these exposures, individual members of the management team began to develop a real commitment to a new managerial strategy. Some of the more "mechanical" improvement activities such as Friday morning improvement meetings were stopped.

Effort was focused on improving team effectiveness in and just below the management team, and on improving intergroup collaboration.

Some real change efforts then began to occur. The vice-president of engineering reorganized his whole function. The work was organized into projects under the direction of project engineers with a high degree of autonomy. The product-planning function was delegated to a product-planning group composed of three members of the managerial team and excluding Mr. C. For expediting new products, task forces on product-management groups were created across divisional lines. Such a group might include the product engineer as chairman, and the production-engineering, scheduling, market-research, and controller's departments. This *middle management* group had the decision-making and action responsibility for getting that product from a research idea to a production item. This represented a major shift in the focus of decision-making.

6. *Education down the Line.*   The management decided to enter into an extensive Managerial Grid program, particularly *Phase One*. It was agreed that the top leadership must participate actively in the conduct of the program. They started with themselves, then with a group of people reporting to them, and worked on down through the organization to and including hourly workers. The entire organization participated in this type of activity over a period of year and a half.

This organization-wide effort did produce some significant changes in the organization climate. Communication across and between levels improved dramatically; long-avoided conflicts were brought out and dealt with. A number of important collaborations developed across departments.

Unfortunately, the follow-up of this educational effort was not as systematic as the educational phase. Over the months, changes and improvements that were recommended by participants in the Grid programs did not materialize. Slowly the feeling began to develop that maybe this was another set of "improvement meetings." On the other hand, the effort had produced enough sense of ownership and participation throughout the organization to have created the impetus for a confrontation with the top management.

From this, better communication and action planning emerged. Further reorganization of functions and additional task forces and temporary systems were set up. A review of the entire compensation policy was initiated which resulted in a creative salary program for the hourly work force including such conditions as pay for time not worked on an excused basis—the same type of criteria traditionally applied to management people.

Further team-building efforts were initiated down the line and a systematic performance improvement program was initiated by and with the top management. Today they set two- and five-year goals and plans. All organization units also set performance and organization-improvement goals.

The top team and each of the divisional teams has an annual self-audit and planning meeting. In terms of "changing the managerial strategy," this goal has been achieved at the top of the organization and is well on the way to achievement in the rest of the management.

Some Results

As a result of the reorganization of the engineering department and the setting up of the task forces between engineering and production, it was possible to bring out, in a period of a year and a half after the beginning of the effort, seven new products or major product changes, whereas in the previous three years, with exactly the same personnel, there had been no major new products. Part of this is a result of previous technical work, but participants in the organization relate this specifically to the organization-improvement effort and to product-management groups which have cut through the interface between production and engineering and are working together toward common goals.

The organization is meeting its profit- and sales-improvement goals at a rate twice as high as before the OD effort began.

The organization has been able to handle 100 percent expansion in volume and two acquisitions with only a minimum increase in manpower.

The morale and satisfaction in the middle management is significantly higher than it was before the change and there has been no loss of key people in middle management. Here is a quote from the president of the company, from a speech in which, after describing the various aspects of his program, he concludes:

> Has this program been helpful? Has our organization changed and, if so, has it been for better or worse? We think the program has helped us grow as a small company in a field of bigs. Sales have increased from 7.6 million to 18 million, with profit increasing as a percent of sales from 5.5 per cent to 6.4 per cent during the past five years. This growth in profit is even more dramatic when you consider that in addition to the cost of the organization-development training

program (about 0.3 per cent of sales) our rate of expenditures for research and development also increased substantially. The growth of the company has been 10 to 15 percent greater than the growth of the industry as a whole over the past five years.

I believe these facts tend to substantiate that a small company must maximize its human potential to survive and grow in a world that is tending toward the "bigs." Secondly, I have tried to illustrate that it has taken me as president about ten years of concentrated effort to change the culture of our company, and we haven't made it all the way yet.

SUMMARY AND ANALYSIS

This case describes a planned attempt to change the top-management style and strategy in an organization from an "authority-obedience" mode, where decisions are made on the basis of hierarchical role, to a participative style or team-management mode, where "ownership" in the company's goals is widely shared; where decisions are made as close as possible to and by the sources of information.

The strategy was to focus first on an in-depth examination of the assumptions, attitudes, and managerial behavior of Mr. C, the president, and his key subordinates. The president, in defining the change problem, was able to see that, as his past efforts showed, just good intentions on his part would not produce these changes in behavior and attitude.

One effort by the consultant was to help the president (an impatient man) see that this change would take time. This effort was not entirely successful with either Mr. C or his top team. As reported, several times during the change effort, executives would enthusiastically install some program (improvement meetings, early Grid activities) without a real commitment to participative problem-solving of the organization's ongoing problems (e.g., new-product development, quality improvement, capacity to react to changing demands in the marketplace).

Similarly, in the early stages, there was a lot of lip service paid to "open communication," "conflict management," and mutual trust, but it was only after a few "crises" that these became part of the internal workings of the top management group. When they developed a real commitment to the new management style, their behavior changed and a number of changes occurred rather quickly: reorganization of work, setting up appropriate task forces, systematic goal-setting at all levels, and improved planning were all introduced and maintained.

The consultant roles in this situation were:

To diagnose the state of the organization with the president;

To counsel with the president;

To counsel with individuals on the management team;

To consult on a regular basis with the management team;

To serve as an educational consultant on individual development plans;

To collect information on organization attitudes;

To be a technician-expert on installing management methods (e.g., performance improvement, target-setting, planning methods).

To convene and manage various intergroup problem-solving activities (e.g., engineering/manufacturing interface, and the top team/product management team interface.

6

A CASE OF CHANGING THE WAY WORK IS DONE

This case illustrates a strategy of organization improvement through redistribution of the work among various parts of the organization.

BACKGROUND

The organization is a major division of a very large chemical company. The policy in recent years is that each of the major divisions operates with high autonomy and freedom. There is a central board at the headquarters and a small central staff. Each division has its own relatively independent management group. The members of these management groups take responsibility for the various operations such as production, engineering, or marketing and also for the various functional units such as personnel, management services, and finance. Reporting to these top managers are a series of operating managers for each of the operations and functions.

This division had been operating for about four years under this model of management. Prior to that time there had been a long history of a paternalistic organization and a favorable profit position. The organization was highly overstaffed, with much duplication. For example, each production unit or plant had a complete engineering department attached to it. There was a tradition in the organization of not firing anyone.

With the problems of a changing economy, the need for considerably higher productivity, very rapidly increasing competition, and the explosion of technology, the organization found its profits slipping and its costs way out of line. It was no longer possible to operate as before—an organization whose products only needed to be produced to be sold.

THE NEED

For several years the personnel director had been systematically introducing behavioral-science concepts into the organization on an experimental basis. He had initiated an experiment in job enrichment using the Herzberg studies as a base.[1] The personnel function itself had been reorganized both in mission and structure. Its mission emphasis had changed from a focus on labor and employee relations to that of human resources planning and development. A number of team development efforts had been started in various sections of the organization.

Several behavioral scientists had visited the organization and met with the top management group to discuss current theory and its application to the division's problems.

The chief executive of the division (we will call him Mr. D) had been in his position for a relatively short time. He was a thoughtful, analytic, and very competent executive, who was familiar with behavioral-science concepts and could see their applications to his organization's concerns.

At the time our case begins, Mr. D and the personnel director were exploring in depth a total organization effort to meet the changing demands for productivity and effectiveness. Some of the priority needs they identified were:

1. A significant increase in productivity.

2. A need for improving the ability of the organization to cope with technical advances. Some new technical equipment had just been introduced and they were having real problems in start-up.

3. The need to reduce the work force by a significant number.

4. The need for changes in function. For example, the need to centralize engineering services so that one engineering organization could provide service to a number of production units on the same site.

---

1   Herzberg, F., et al. The Motivation to Work. New York: John Wiley & Sons, 1959.

Another example—the need to reduce the levels of supervision and provide more freedom and autonomy for supervisors at various levels.

5. The need for relocating decisions throughout the organization.

INITIAL DIAGNOSIS AND STRATEGY

The personnel director brought a behavioral-science consultant to the division headquarters for a few days to further discuss the organization problems with Mr. D and other key executives and to explore possible ways of working on them. The consultant spent some time with the personnel department, the top management group, the head of manufacturing, and the engineering services group. These discussions indicated the following:

1. A need for change in the workings of the top group; they were involved in both policy and operational direction, to the detriment of both and to the frustration of operating managers.

2. A need for creating a different work climate in the top team. Communication was closed and members were very status-conscious and politic in their behavior toward each other. This behavior was part of the culture of the parent company.

3. A need for getting more decisions moved down the line at all levels.

4. A need for reducing the layers of supervision in the production area.

5. A need for combining the engineering services and a corollary need for developing a climate of cooperation between engineering and production. Mutual distrust was the present condition.

6. A need to create more collaboration between the shop-floor work force and foremen. Related to this was the low status of foremen as perceived by both workers and management.

From this analysis a change strategy was developed by Mr. D and the personnel director. It was then presented to the top team and, upon their agreement, went into effect. Initial efforts would include:

1. An examination and restatement of the organization's goals by the top management.

2. An examination of the management group's functions with the goal of reorganizing the work so that as a *management* group they focused

on policy development and planning and not on day-to-day operations.

3. A reorganization of the composition of the management team, if indicated after the functional analysis.

4. The movement of operating decisions to the operating managers.

5. A reduction of force.

   a)   Experiments to be conducted in two large plants reducing levels of supervision and combining functions.

   b)   A program developed to prepare managements of these plants for the change. They should be given major responsibility for managing the change efforts with support from top manufacturing management.

   c)   Team development efforts for the "new" team.

6. The combining of engineering services.

   a)   A development program with the engineering-services management group.

   b)   An intergroup conference between engineering-services management and plant managers to deal with attitudes toward the "merger."

   c)   The creation of an interorganization liaison group to help with the changeover.

ACTIONS

The first year's major action steps were with the management group.

1. Mr. D wrote an updated statement of division objectives. This was discussed, modified and published by the division management team.

2. Mr. D did an analysis of agenda items handled by the group in the last six months. The group working from this decided which agenda should be handled by them and which should be delegated to other functions.

3. The group examined its own organization and reorganized in a more flexible mode.

   a)   For policy decisions and planning, there was one configuration (the original group).

b)   For periodic performance reviews, a much smaller group (Mr. D, financial head, business area heads).

c)   For operational management, short-term, the original group plus the operating heads (next level down).

4. They built in a periodic review system to evaluate the effectiveness of the revised functioning.

5. The chief executive and one deputy attended a laboratory for presidents. Subsequently all members of the group attended similar programs.

6. It was recognized that there was inadequate competence in goal-setting. A specific goal-setting procedure was introduced for fiscal and financial planning and also for manpower and organization planning.

Starting concurrently with the above steps for the management group, work was begun with the manufacturing organization, which contained by far the largest number of people in the entire organization. The head of manufacturing attended a laboratory in human behavior, and a management team was built composed of the various plant managers plus a small manufacturing staff. Up to that time, all relationships had been of individual plants disconnected from each other and reporting to the manufacturing manager. They now became a manufacturing-management operation. Plant managers who were engaged in change or improvement efforts, such as the reduction of levels of supervision, a change in structure, or a change in the ways of work, began developing change-management teams. People were appointed as change agents working collaboratively with the change manager or the manager of the unit.

After about eight months, a one-week workshop was conducted for *teams* of change agents, teams composed of a plant manager and his personnel man. At the workshop, in addition to sessions on the theory of change and change-planning, the participants worked on their own specific change projects. Projects included plant-productivity improvement programs, reductions in force, developing more participative management, and changing roles and functions in a plant.

The engineering-services group set up a series of interorganization meetings with plant managers to find ways of increasing collaboration and reducing the conflict between the groups. An interdepartmental management group was set up to continue "managing" the change.

Some results after a two-year period were:

1. The organization significantly reduced the size of its work force, with an increase in efficiency. Many jobs and functions were relocated.

2. In most plants, there are two levels less of supervision than at the beginning of the change effort, with no loss of productivity or efficiency.

3. More than 30 percent of the agenda previously handled and decided at the top level is now decided at a lower management level.

4. In terms of plans for 1970 sales and profit targets, this division's goal, originally set several years previously, was raised significantly. The management has recently concluded an organization-wide goal-setting exercise, as a result of which they have committed for a target higher than the one originally asked for by the corporate headquarters.

SUMMARY AND ANALYSIS

This case illustrates a strategy of focusing on the organization of work as a primary factor in organization improvement. As in all the cases described, there is no pure strategy. In this case there was a change in culture and in managerial strategy, but the major focus was on work organization and methods.

The strategy was to focus first on the *work* of the top management group. As an early step in the change effort, they reallocated the work among themselves and their subordinates.

Other reallocations or "reorganizations," such as combining the engineering-services function and expanding the personnel function, were major aspects of the OD effort. These relocations of work produced needs for retraining of management, for establishing new relations, for examining and working on interpersonal and intergroup communications, and for resetting unit objectives. New teams were created which produced a need for team-development activities.

Significant changes in organization climate developed in this case. The strategy for achieving the new condition was to develop a collaborative team effort toward more effective *work* organization.

The consultant roles in this case included:

An initial assessment of the "state of things" through discussions with representative managers throughout the organization.

A "comparison assessment"—the consultant's picture compared with the client's (Mr. D's and the personnel director's) picture of things.

Consultation on methods and tactics (analysis of management-group agenda; plan for conferences between engineering and plant management).

Consultation with key executives (Mr. D, personnel director, manufacturing director).

Consultation with teams (management group, manufacturing management, engineering-services group, personnel managers).

Training (courses for change agents).

Education consultation (development programs, e.g., laboratories, management courses at universities, for executives).

7

A CASE OF CREATIVE ADAPTATION
TO A NEW ENVIRONMENT

This case illustrates an organization strategy for adjustment to a new environment. It also describes the use of a pilot project as a strategy to initiate and develop a total organization change.

BACKGROUND

The case concerns a large investment and commercial bank. Due to the changing pressures of the environment and increasing competition, the top management had decided that it must build up its public banking business. This decision meant the addition of numbers of branch banks. There was also an explosion of activity in the handling of large personal and pension trusts.

Historically, the bank had been managed in a benevolent, autocratic mode, with low pay, good benefits, supervision of varied quality, a class society, very limited communication, and very direct supervision at the lower levels.

The top management of the organization felt that something should be done to upgrade the quality of supervision at middle management levels in order to increase productivity. They also planned to introduce more modern systems in order to keep up with the changing demands and requirements of the times. A sophisticated management-methods organization was developed; studies were made throughout the bank to determine where to introduce electronic data-processing; supervisory work methods were analyzed and improvements recommended. Some of the efforts to introduce new methods were not working particularly well due to a high degree of resistance among old-line managers at all levels but particularly in middle management.

THE NEED

The personnel management was aware of the need for a major change in the whole atmosphere of the organization, if any significant improvement was to occur. Turnover rates were extremely high. The bank had been able to recruit good men from the better colleges, but recently had been losing them after the first few years at an alarming rate. In very recent years the actual recruitment had dropped. The bank just didn't seem to be an exciting place for high-potential young people out of college to come to work. In recent years, also, there had been an increasing number of resignations of effective middle managers. Although the top management was quite concerned about the climate, in their minds the problem clearly lay in the behavior of middle management.

The personnel people felt that an essential first condition, if real improvement was to occur, was for the top management to look at its own attitudes, style, behavior, and philosophy. They felt there would have to be a change in the attitudes and values at the top if anything significant were to occur in the middle.

Over a period of two years a number of strategies had been considered or tried by the "change agents" in personnel. First, there had been some discussions about starting a program with the top managers. The response had been, "As we've told you, the problem is not with us; we know we've got difficulties in the organization or we wouldn't be after you to fix them. The problem is with the middle management—go and work with them."

A second strategy that had been considered was to initiate an attitude survey on the assumption that the data it would produce would make clear to top management the things they needed to do (i.e., start with themselves). After testing this possible strategy with some outside consultants, the personnel people decided not to try this. They realized that there was a strong likelihood that such a report might simply increase the resistance and defensiveness of top management, rather than getting them to move.

A third strategy that was tried was to expose the top management, in a non-threatening way, to some of the advanced thinking about organization values, motivation, and effectiveness. Luncheons were set up with some of the leading thinkers in the field. The management's response to this effort showed that it felt these were interesting meetings and very informative but the inputs were somewhat theoretical and not particularly applicable to the bank's situation.

A fourth strategy was to arrange for exposure of the top management to counterpart top managers in organizations known to them. Those selected headed organizations that had engaged in a planned organization-improvement program with some success. The stories of these efforts and favorable results impressed the top management of the bank, but they did not see a direct application from other types of industry and business to their own situation.

About eighteen months after the first attempts, a fifth strategy emerged. This was to suggest a pilot project—an action experiment—to see if significant difference could be made in the climate, operating effectiveness, and productivity of a small segment of the organization through a planned "intervention," as a basis for considering larger efforts. Top management was willing to support such an experiment and the total change effort was started.

INITIAL DIAGNOSIS AND STRATEGY

The personnel leadership used a variety of outside help during the process. In their early attempt to do an attitude survey, they turned to some specialists in survey research methods who actually designed the survey.

The man from the personnel department who was in charge of the effort attended a workshop on organization change. From the other participants and from the staff of the workshop, he got help in thinking through the consequences of the survey, and from this he made the decision not to go ahead with it.

In their third strategy, they used "expert" resources, relying on an "appreciation session" to mobilize the interest of the top group.

After the fourth strategy, they brought in a consultant (there was a previous relationship from the workshop) and began to develop a fifth strategy—the pilot project.

Looking at the organization, the following facts were clear:

1. Ultimately, the top management would have to accept the responsibility to become personally involved in examining their strategy, policies, reward systems, and managerial behavior.

2. This ultimate condition was not where top management was at this time, and there was low readiness to move there.

3. In order for top management to see the relevance of this type of self-examination, they would have to see some evidence of the effectiveness of change efforts in the organization.

4. Top management felt that changes should occur in the "middle" of the organization. Therefore, they would be "interested" in successful changes at that level.

5. There was a clear need for people in the middle of the organization to have more influence on decisions and better communication with the top.

6. Any early efforts must be successful in top management's eyes, if further efforts were to have a chance.

7. A relatively small "intervention," with a group somewhere down the line where there was a felt problem, could produce this success and perhaps lead to further experimentation and programming.

Given these "facts" the personnel people decided to try to develop a pilot project. A suborganization would be located and an "improvement" activity would be started with this group.

It was also planned to measure the change effort so that top management would have some basis for determining the effects of such efforts on performance and productivity. Therefore, in addition to the "pilot group," a couple of control groups would need to be identified.

It was planned to use a time period of one year for the measurement so that enough time could elapse for a change to be made and somewhat stabilized.

It was decided to have one outside consultant work with the pilot group and to have an independent research effort conducted by another outside organization. A research team from a nearby university was selected.

Management would be asked to support this specific pilot project and to commit itself to a study of the results.

ACTIONS

The components of the pilot project were as follows:

In the trust division of the organization there were three groups whose work was heavily interdependent. Relationships and work effectiveness were not very satisfactory in any of these groups. In addition each group had attached to it a staff of methods specialists whose mission was to try to help the group upgrade its work methods. As part of a bank-wide plan, much of the work currently handled through mechanized bookkeeping was about to be put on a computer. The methods group had the specific task of getting the computer installed and operating in the operations group.

It was decided to engage in a one-year project with a team composed of the managements of these two groups. The stated purposes were to improve their operating effectiveness as a problem-solving unit and to facilitate the introduction of the computer into pension operations.

The team engaged in the pilot project was made up of nine managers from the operating group and three from the methods group. We will call this group the "experimental team." The steps taken with the experimental team included planned preparation of both the individuals and the team before the first of three off-site meetings.

1. Each of the members of the team went to a sensitivity-training laboratory.

2. The team members met with the consultant for a half-day. He described the goals of the project and the possible outcomes. He asked each member of the experimental group to submit an anonymous letter to him listing the obstacles to more effective operation of this team, of the environment around this team, and of the total bank.

3. The consultant organized the information from the letters as a basis for initial analysis with the team.

4. The team then went away for its first weekend conference. The consultant started the meeting by reporting back the summary of information from the letters.

The group then reviewed the list of problems, set priorities, and began to work on them. These problems included such items as:

a)   Style of the supervisor of the group.

b)   Relationships between the supervisor and his section heads.

c)   Relationships between the operations group and the methods specialists.

d)   The status (perceived low) of this group compared to other groups in the bank.

e)   Relationships between this group and bank management.

As a result of the individual exposure to the sensitivity-training and because of the large number of real problems and the *fact* of the meeting, there was high commitment among members to confront the problems and to try to improve the state of affairs. Discussions were frank, open, and sometimes painful.

By the end of the weekend the group had decided:

a)   To continue meeting monthly at the bank (without a consultant).

b)   To set up three task forces to work on some internal problems.

c)   To have the supervisor of operations call a meeting of his two counterparts to set up an ongoing interdepartmental-communications mechanism.

d)   To contact central personnel for some help in cleaning up some personnel-methods problems.

5. The team did meet monthly and carried out most of their action plans.

6. Six months later the second weekend conference was held with the consultant attending. This meeting was planned by the team. They had an agenda of priority problems that required more time than was available in their monthly meetings. They worked the agenda and set action plans for the following six months. One decision was to cut down on meetings of the group. They appointed a steering committee of three people who were authorized to appoint task forces of "resources" from the group to work on specific problems.

7. The total group met again six months later with the consultant to review the year's work and assess future needs. They decided that there was no further need for meetings of this group for a year because work was being handled through appropriate task forces.

They decided there *was* a need for the group to meet as a group with the administration group to work on ways of increasing collaboration and communication between the two organizations.

The Measurement of the Project

The research was conducted by a team from a university and consisted of the following components:

1. Subordinates of the experimental team members and of the counterparts in the control teams were interviewed on their attitudes toward the organization, their section, and their boss' behavior. These interviews were conducted before the first team meeting and one year later.

2. Members of the team were interviewed at the end of the year as to what changes they saw as having taken place and why.

3. The man in charge of the area of work which included the experimental team and the counterpart teams was interviewed before and after on the effectiveness of each of the groups.

4. Some other managers at higher levels who had periodic contact with the experimental group were interviewed before and after on their perceptions of the group's effectiveness.

5. Productivity measures such as personnel turnover and work measurement were recorded for both the experimental and control groups.

6. The consultant wrote a report at the end of the year on his perception of the changes.

These several types of data were collected separately with no contact between data collectors. The material was then coordinated by a member of the university research team and produced in a report which was presented to the management of the bank.

Results

This report indicated some dramatic changes in the effectiveness of the experimental group in both its productivity and its working methods. As a result the two other related groups in the division mentioned previously began similar programs of team development. The leaders of the three interrelated groups became a permanent management team for coordination purposes.

A similar team was developed at the section-manager level among the three units. Some other new communications mechanisms were set up between the organizations, such as closed circuit television for weekly joint conferences. The original group and one of the others held an intergroup meeting to work through a number of relationship problems which had emerged from the two individual team-development programs. These two groups together then met with representatives of the third group to work through some additional relationship and procedural problems.

Some new relationships were established between this division and the corporate staff of the bank, particularly the personnel department.

The senior vice-president in charge of this entire area began some team-development activities with his key subordinates.

One year after the end of the experiment, the top thirty managers in the organization went away for a four-day workshop to look at their own functioning and its effects on the total bank effort. Outputs of that top-management meeting included a change in the recruitment structure, the development of a management-trainee posture, some changes in the reward system for young men, and the appointment of task forces to examine the entire reward system. A bank-wide management-training program, including the Managerial Grid and laboratory training, was established.

Today, there is a consulting group who work with various units in the bank. Off-site team-development meetings of operating units are now a regular part of the operating mode.

A major result was that the top management, which was not approachable through any of the earlier strategies, did see (based in large part on the results of the pilot-project effort and the changes that it produced) the need for taking some bank-wide looks at their managerial strategy. In terms of the outputs of the specific change-effort described above, the following excerpt is quoted from the report prepared by the researchers (based on interviews with the experimental-team members at the end of the year).[1]

1   In order to protect the anonymity of the organization, the source of the research report is not being disclosed.

"Positive changes were described in detail, and many different sources were indicated for these changes. For instance, the following types of favorable changes were indicated:

structural changes in the makeup of sections,
increased communication among team members,
increased concern on the part of all to be of help to one another,
better decision making,
increased satisfaction,
increased expectation of promotional opportunities,
increased respect for senior officers.

The perceived sources of these changes emanate from the following:

the inception of team training,
changes in self during sensitivity training,
changes in self as a result of learning how to supervise more appropriately,
changes in the senior officers (and the transfer of one particular officer).

The management team (of the experimental group) has definite perceptions of having shifted in the direction of giving more freedom and using a more general approach to supervision as illustrated by the following comments:

"One supervisor says of his boss (who's also in the team) 'We have more freedom to go to him—he has opened his door, he is tolerant, considerate, and willing to give an attentive ear to our ideas.'

"Another respondent says of the same person, 'I can say things now I wouldn't have dared to say a year ago. I can tell him he's wrong and he will listen.'

"A third respondent says about another boss, 'We used to have to check every bit of work activity with our superiors; now we go ahead and do it, keeping them informed of what we're doing.'

"One manager relates the following example, 'About four weeks ago, a customer was going to start a new plan. It usually takes four or five months to develop this plan. In the past, I would have started making assignments to individuals to construct the plan according to my specifications. In this instance, I called in my supervisors, told them the problem, told them it had to be done in two months, and asked them how they thought it should be done. Each one offered his own resources, allotted extra time for certain personnel; one man volunteered a person from his staff to work up a plan, and another set up a production schedule which will allow us to finish on time. It was great—they completely handled the responsibility.' "

In interviewing upper managers and counterpart managers, the major changes reported were more cooperation, better efficiency, and better capacity to cope with complexity. A typical quote was:

"They are more sympathetic, more anxious to accommodate. A major reorganization was handled between two divisions with virtually no problems."

A report from another officer:

"I also noticed an increased tendency for the division people to take a more universal view of problems than they had before. They no longer try to place blame on someone—they try to do what's best for all."

In addition to this kind of evidence, productivity data of various kinds were accumulated. A few of those results:

"As of the end of the third quarter (prior to the change effort) the division had higher days lost per individual and higher percentage of absenteeism than the control divisions. However, by the end of the following year this picture showed a striking difference. The division was lowest in days lost and in percentage of absenteeism. The relative changes expressed as a percentage increase or decrease show this quite sharply. The division showed clear improvement, while control group one stayed fairly steady and control group two showed a clear drop."

Another quote:

"Productivity data supplied by the work-measurement division include proof that, first, the division became, over the period of the study, much more cooperative with the work-analysis program, less defensive, and more actively interested in systematic work measurement as a means of assessing the productivity of their own personnel. Secondly, they (the work-study men) point out that the division showed an increase in effectiveness over the period studied, while in the two control groups, one showed no increased effectiveness or a decrease while the other group's effectiveness remained relatively constant. Thus, it seems reasonably clear that productivity as measured in this fashion shows an increase in the experimental group but not in the controls."

The conclusion of this research study states:

1. *Productivity Orientation.* The consultant's report, the productivity data, and the observations of the work-measurement staff, all support the idea that team members became more oriented toward productivity.

2. *Work Attractiveness.* The survey data show with reasonable clarity that the division employees came to like their work more during the period of the study.

3. *Autonomy.* Improved attitudes toward work usually stem not only from the nature of the work itself (which in this study did not change) but from the interpersonal relations between superiors, subordinates, and peers. The survey data show quite clearly that the division subordinates saw their work setting as providing more autonomy (less pressure, less close supervision, more time to be friendly with peers), and their perceptions of their section heads' behavior were congruent with this view. In most of the management team's own views, the themes of less work pressure and more autonomy are very clear.

4. *Upward Influence.* This autonomy was not sheer laissez-faire withdrawal from responsibility. Both the interviews with the team and the survey of employees stressed increased upward influence both in a general way and on the specific issue of promotions. Thus, the relative ability of managers involved in the project to participate effectively in decision-making with their superiors has been seen to increase.

5. *Openness.* Implicit in the idea of increased upward influence is the necessity for full, trustful communication across levels. In the consultant's report, the interviews with the team members and the comments of the work-measurement staff all suggest that the team became more able to give and receive data freely about ongoing problems than before.

6. *Collaborative Orientation and Skills.* The consultants report that the interviews with the managers themselves and the interviews with the

managers outside the team all stress the team members' increased ability to tackle and solve problems with others on an even status basis.

7. Bank-Wide Orientation. Reports and interviews with associated managers agreed that the team had become much more oriented to the good of the firm as a whole. This appeared to have several related components—an increase in objectivity, an increase in problem orientation, and an increase in universalism.

8. Development Orientation. Finally, the interviews with the team indicate a shift in the direction of increased concern with self-development, with the extension of the team concept to other parts of the bank, and with the training orientation and development of subordinates.

It was this information that was one major force in motivating upper management of the bank to move ahead toward a total bank-wide organization-improvement effort.

SUMMARY AND ANALYSIS

This case illustrates a strategy for coping with changes in the external environment which require changing the internal environment. It shows the strategy of using a pilot project with highly visible results as a way of starting an organization-wide change effort.

An issue in this case is the problem of different perceptions among managers in the organization of the nature of the "illness," and of the type of "treatment" indicated. Lacking data or experience, action decisions tend to be made on the basis of organization role.

By introducing a specific experiment or *pilot intervention* and letting it spread out through related parts of the organization, managers at all levels could *see* the results and were thus willing to commit themselves to further "experiments" such as the top management retreat (which is now a regular affair).

The consultant roles in this case included:

Providing expertise in survey-feedback methods (early strategy not used).

Consultation on strategies for working with top management.

Educational consultation on development activities (Grids, laboratory training).

Educational expertise (presentation to top management in early strategies and presentation for authorization of pilot project).

Consulting with teams on methods and team-building (experimental team/top management team).

Consultant on intergroup conferences.

Consultant to top managers (after pilot project, on follow-up strategies).

Consultant and trainer of internal resources (personnel staff, etc.).

Link to other behavioral science resources.

Consulting team providing periodic organization-health assessments in collaboration with bank management.

8

A CASE OF CHANGING COMMUNICATIONS
AND INFLUENCE PATTERNS

This case illustrates a strategy for developing trust and effective communication between staff/line and headquarters/field groups.

BACKGROUND

The organization in this case is a large, extremely successful, marketing-oriented consumer-products company, with a rather extensive production and manufacturing organization. There are large production plants producing similar types of products located in various parts of the country.

The managers of these plants report to division managers who are physically located in the central headquarters city but are responsible for groups of plants in some regional area. These division managers report to a head of manufacturing.

To service the plants, there are a number of staff divisions located in the headquarters city. There is an industrial engineering staff which furnishes methods improvement, work study, organization analysis, and information systems. There is also an industrial relations staff which is concerned with training, management development, recruitment, employee and labor relations, and compensation.

The staffs in the headquarters had had continuing problems in the past of maintaining "clients" in the plants, and of introducing their techniques and technologies to the manufacturing organization. Such techniques and technologies were not always welcomed by the field managers. There was also a certain amount of competition between the various staff divisions, particularly those concerned with introducing organization change.

THE NEED

The need for this particular organization-wide change effort was originally felt by one of the division managers in the manufacturing organization. He had received a lot of input from his plant managers about the poor relationships between the plants and the headquarters staffs. Plant managers complained of a lack of service and inadequate support from the central office. Simultaneously, a need was reported for better coordination of efforts among the operations-research, industrial-engineering, and the personnel and development staffs. The division manager checked with his counterparts and found similar attitudes existed throughout the manufacturing organization. He contacted the heads of the various staffs. Working with an internal consultant (a member of the personnel staff whose function was to facilitate organization-improvement efforts) he developed an overall strategy. Outside consultant help was brought in to assist with the diagnosis and change program.

INITIAL DIAGNOSIS AND STRATEGY

The analysis indicated the following:

1. A need for establishing intergroup collaboration and a better working relationship between the industrial-relations and the industrial-engineering groups.

2. A need for the examination of the system of rewards to both these staff groups. The rewards had been pretty much for services rendered in their own specialty. No rewards were given for collaborative work with another unit.

3. A recognition that there was a lot of capability in both staff organizations and that many of the skills overlapped. An agreement that a team approach with a combination of operations-research and behavioral-science capabilities could, in many instances, do the best diagnosis and give best assistance to field problems.

4. A need for upgrading the personnel or human-resources function in the plants to decrease the dependency on the headquarters.

5. A need for plant managers and division managers to examine their own styles relative to the management of human resources.

6. A need for some joint problem-solving by the field managements and the headquarters staffs.

7. A possible need for some new forms of organizing the way services were called for and provided.

From this analysis the following strategies were developed:

1. There should be some internal team-building efforts within the staffs to get their own self-images clear.

2. There should be some intergroup work between industrial-relations and industrial-engineering to search for common goals and ways of increasing collaborative effort.

3. There should be some further information-collection from plant managers on their needs and problems.

4. The division managers should examine the quality of the personnel function in the plants as a basis for developing improved capability in each plant.

5. There should be some joint activity between representatives of plant and division management and representatives of industrial-relations management to work on the issues between the groups and to look for ways of improved collaboration and service.

6. Top manufacturing management and top staff management should periodically review the state of the relationships and the work.

ACTIONS

The following actions occurred:

1. The industrial-relations group held a couple of team-building programs to work on their own interpersonal relations and team effectiveness.

2. Members of this team attended advanced programs in training and/or organization development to upgrade their technical capability.

3. Meetings were started on a regular basis between the department heads of the industrial-engineering group concerned with organization development and with the department heads of the industrial-relations staff.

Several joint meetings were held with an outside consultant and the total membership of both groups, to examine their relationships and problems, to work on the development of common goals, and to improve work methods.

4. One division manager, at this regular semiannual management meeting, devoted the majority of the meeting to an assessment of the problems and obstacles toward improved performance that grew out of the relationship between the field organization and the staff organizations at headquarters. The output of this was shared with the other division managers and the manufacturing manager and with the head of industrial relations.

5. A three-day, off-site meeting was held between industrial relations and manufacturing management. Attending were the head of industrial relations; the heads of the employee relations, training and development, recruitment, and compensation sections from the industrial-relations group; and three of the four division managers and seven of the sixteen plant managers from the manufacturing organization.

At this meeting the field people shared their image of, and attitudes about, the industrial-relations staff. Conversely, the staff people expressed their frustrations and problems with the manufacturing people. A list of priority issues was produced and ways for handling each of the issues were developed. The outputs of this meeting included:

a) A major reorganization of the services to the field: from within the industrial-relations group, the employee-relations people were des-ignated as "account executives," each to have liaison responsibility with a specific number of plants or field operations. Their major mission was redefined as: to be available to plant management for the diagnosis and development of priority concerns for improvement within the plant and for the provision of appropriate technical support from both the industrial-relations and the industrial-engineering staffs.

b) To help prepare the employee-relations people for this change role, a specialist who was highly skilled and trained in organization-development was assigned full time to this group to help them upgrade their technical capability, and to be available as a consultant to them in their relations with the field.

c) Steps were undertaken to upgrade the quality of personnel in that role.

d) Follow-up meetings were arranged between the various groups. A timetable was developed for introduction of these changes, division by division.

6. One division management, in order to facilitate the organization-development program, assigned a number of managers (both line and staff) to be "change agents." Their assignment was to provide help to units of the division engaged in various change efforts. They were to assist in team-development activities, improve intergroup collaboration, and improve planning.

This group is engaged in an intensive self-development program, using behavioral-science consultants from a university staff.

7. More members of the industrial-engineering and the industrial-relations staff are attending advanced-training programs in this field.

8. A coordinating organization composed of line people representing four levels of management, plus the leadership of the various staff organizations, has been created. It functions as a task force to maintain perspective on, and continue the forward development of, the entire change effort in the manufacturing area. This group meets quarterly with two behavioral-science organization consultants.

SUMMARY AND ANALYSIS

This case represents an example of a change in communications and influence patterns toward increased organization effectiveness. The strategy included:

an identification of the subsystems (plant management, industrial relations staff, etc.) who had relationship problems;

strengthening their own internal functioning;

bringing top management representatives from interfacing units together;

bringing full membership of interfacing units into joint problem solving activities;

creating new organization forms (account executive) to meet changing needs.

The consultant roles in this case included:

Diagnosis of relevant subsystems.

Consulting with change managers (division manager, head of industrial relations).

Procedural consultant to intergroup meetings (plant-management/industrial relations; industrial-relations/industrial-engineering).

Consultant to teams in team-development (industrial-relations; industrial-engineering; divisional-manufacturing group).

Methods consultation on new organization forms (account executive model).

Trainer of internal resources (training and OD specialists; account executives).

Catalyst between field and headquarters managements.

9
CONDITIONS FOR FAILURE AND SUCCESS
IN ORGANIZATION-DEVELOPMENT EFFORTS

In this chapter I want to look at some of the conditions that can get in the way of effective organization improvement, and then at some of the conditions necessary for a successful, lasting change effort.

SOME CONDITIONS FOR FAILURE

1. A continued discrepancy between top management statements of values and styles and their actual managerial behavior.

I know of one organization which has spent considerable money and effort over several years in organization-improvement efforts. The effectiveness of the organization is only marginally increased. The top management still operates in a generally autocratic and sometimes crisis-oriented style. The rest of the organization knows this, and has only limited trust in the statements of intention from the top. There is a credibility gap which causes people to be cautious, conservative and self-protective.

2. A big program of activities without any solid base of change goals.

Some organization managers install activities such as management laboratories, a piece of a Managerial Grid program, or a "package" of goal-setting activities, and assume this to be an OD program. They don't have a personal commitment to the systematic setting of goals and plans for achieving them and to providing responsible leadership in organization improvement.

3. Confusion of ends and means.

Some managers, having had a significant personal learning experience in a program, say, of sensitivity training, will sincerely promote a program of attendance at such activities by their colleagues, on the assumption that personal development of key managers will *ipso facto* result in organization improvement. Unless the question "training for what?" can be answered in organization-development terms, such means will not improve *organization* effectiveness.

4. Short time framework.

Most top managers are activists; they are results-oriented and impatient. One condition that can doom OD efforts is an unrealistic expectation of short-term results. Even if dramatic short-run changes do occur, they are not a valid measure of real organization improvement. Three to five years is a realistic time frame in which an OD effort may be expected to show meaningful results.

5. No connection between behavioral-science-oriented change efforts and management-services/operations-research-oriented change efforts.

There are a number of systematic efforts to change the operations of organizations that are not coordinated at the staff level. These produce inefficiencies and competition between staffs and do not take advantage of the synergy that is possible in a joint effort to systematically plan and conduct a change in the organization.

6. Overdependence on outside help.

With the increasing complexity of organizations and of the demands of the environment, it is easy to let consultants or specialists "solve the problem." In organization-development efforts this is not a long-term, useful strategy. The management of the organization must have a continuing personal commitment to the problems and to their solutions.

7. Overdependence on inside specialists.

This is a similar condition where the line management lets the change effort be handled entirely by the organization or staff specialists.

8. A large gap between the change effort at the top of the organization and efforts in the middle of the organization.

Frequently, the top-management group will engage in major effort to improve its functioning, operations, and work. This takes time and energy. During the time of this effort, there may well be an increase in communications problems and social distance between the top group and the middle of the organization. If the changes at the top are not communicated and transferred to the next layer of organization, it is difficult to achieve an integrated organization-development effort.

9. Trying to fit a major organization change into an old structure.

Some organization-development efforts have failed because managers have tried to fit some changed conditions, such as a new marketing strategy or a reorientation of effort, into an existing structure. For example, in a large advertising agency, clients had contact with the agency through the account executive. The various specialists in media and art, etc., worked through this executive. Today, the clients want to make direct contact with the various specialists for the several parts of their advertising program. By maintaining the old structure and internal relationships, the agency experienced difficulty in dealing with client needs. Only when they realized that a new structure was necessary to cope with the change in the environment were they able to handle this problem creatively.

10. Confusing "good relationships" as an *end* with good relationships as a *condition.*

Some behavioral-science organization-change programs imply that when effective, open, trusting relationships exist among the people of the organization, you have organization health. They imply that an end goal of such a program is to establish this type of climate and relationships. They do not indicate that the effective, healthy organization, in addition to good relationships, has clear goals and definite plans for achieving them, and that the suborganizations are also working against goals. Good relationships are an important condition in an effective organization but they are not an *end state.*

11. The search for "cookbook" solutions.

There are still many managers who will try anything that will provide a quick solution to improving the organization's effectiveness. Real organization health is not subject to cookbook solutions.

12. Applying an intervention or strategy inappropriately.

There are a number of cases in my own experience where a particular intervention or change strategy which was effective in one organization or under one set of conditions, has been borrowed and applied to another organization or set of conditions without any diagnosis as to its appropriateness in the second organization. This is a form of cookbook solution and it tends to produce failure rather than success.

SOME CONDITIONS FOR SUCCESS

In an article in the Harvard Business Review,[1] Larry Greiner reports on a study of a number of successful organization-change efforts on which research was done. He has analyzed the reports of the researchers, and has been able to select from these reports a set of common characteristics that pertain to all the successful change efforts and were not present in the less successful ones. Here is his list:

1. There is pressure on the top management which induces some arousal to action.

2. There is some form of intervention at the top, either a new member of the organization, or a consultant, or a new staff head in organization-development. This induces some reorientation in looking at internal problems.

3. There is a diagnosis of the problem areas and this induces an analysis of specific problems.

4. There is an invention of some new solutions to problems and this produces some commitment to new courses of action.

5. There is some experimentation with new solutions and this produces a search for results with the experiments.

6. There is reinforcement in the system from positive results and this produces acceptance of the new practices.

---

1   Greiner, L. E. "Patterns of Organization Change." *Harv. Bus. Rev.,* **45,** No. 3, May-June, 1967.

The reader might find it useful to look at the cases in Chapters 4 through 8 and test them against these criteria.

My own list of ten conditions necessary for successful organization development efforts follows:

1. There is pressure from the environment, internal or external, for change.

2. Some strategic person or people are "hurting."

3. Some strategic people are willing to do a real diagnosis of the problem.

4. There is leadership (consultant, key staff man, new line executive).

5. There is collaborative problem identification between line and staff people.

6. There is some willingness to take risks in trying new forms or relationships.

7. There is a realistic, long-term time perspective.

8. There is a willingness to face the data of the situation and to work with it on changing the situation.

9. The system rewards people for the *effort* of changing and improvement, in addition to rewarding them for short-term results.

10. There are tangible intermediate results.

We will move on in the next chapter to look at the management of organization development in terms of line management and staff and consultant support.

PART 3

MANAGING CHANGE

10

THE MANAGEMENT OF ORGANIZATION DEVELOPMENT

Let me recall for the reader my definition of organization development.

Organization development is an effort (1) *planned*, (2) *organization-wide*, and (3) *managed* from the *top*, to (4) increase *organization effectiveness* and *health* through (5) *planned interventions* in the organization's "processes," using *behavioral-science* knowledge.

The goals of all organization-development efforts are improved effectiveness in performance and improved organization health with the ability to remain effective.

The success of organization-development efforts is in large part related to the quality of the management of the efforts and the commitment of the top management of the organization to invest the necessary energy and personal effort.

This chapter will look at the management of organization-development efforts.

We will look first at some models of initiating OD efforts within the line organization; then move to an analysis of the kinds of outside help available to organization leaders in terms of both consultants and programs; and finally look at several models of organizing the internal staff resources for assisting in the management of change.

Two terms appropriate in this exploration are "change managers" and "change agents." The first refers to those people, such as the chief executive of the organization or the head of a unit, who are responsible for the organization's operations and effectiveness, and who must accept major management responsibility in any planned organization or unit-wide change effort. "Change agent" refers to those people, either inside or outside the organization, who are providing technical, specialist, or consulting assistance in the management of a change effort. They may be providing staff work in planning the effort; they may be collecting information on the state of the system; they may be providing technical help in training and consulting; they may be serving as diagnosticians for the line management. A professional role of "change agent" is beginning to emerge in organization-development work. I think we will see more of this role in the years to come.

CHANGE MANAGEMENT

Although most would agree that any organization-wide change must be "owned" and managed by the top leadership of the organization, this condition is not always possible at the start of a change effort. In organization-wide efforts there are a number of ways of initiating change which have proved effective. Let me describe a few.

1. *The Chief Executive as the OD Director.* Sometimes the chief executive or top manager of the organization decides to undertake and manage an organization-wide change program. He usually arrives at this decision based on some personal experience or referral from a respected source. He may see the gaps between the present operation of his organization and his image of what it might be. For example, he might want to change the quality and perhaps the type of goals set by the organization, or the way the organization operates, or the structure, or the climate. In this situation, because of his position and because people in such positions are usually high-energy people, he may use his power to push the program along fairly quickly.

This could result in a number of activities; his behavior could communicate to the organization that this is the "game"—people will be rewarded for engaging in improvement activities. It could also mean that any resistance to change within the organization would be reduced because of the top-management support.

Enthusiasm and personal commitment from the top leadership can be one of the strongest forces for an effective change program. However, this situation is not without some disadvantages. Some of the heavy commitment from the top manager might not be shared by those immediately below him although they would "go along." There might well be a lag in commitment and action between the efforts of the top-management group and the people reporting to them. I have seen a number of situations in which the top team, sparked by the enthusiasm of the president, became extremely committed to an improvement program but this commitment did not carry on to the level immediately below them. In one case that comes to mind, the president is a real enthusiast for planned organization improvement. He and his top team spend approximately three times as much time together working on such problems as they did before. For a period of over a year, however, the top team has been considerably less available to their subordinates. There is increasing dissatisfaction at the operating-head level about the lack of contact with the executive group. There are some rather serious morale problems in the middle of the organization and a mounting degree of hostility toward "the program." The OD effort is seen as getting in the way of organization effectiveness rather than improving it. Another problem may occur when the chief executive, having become committed to a particular program, decides that it should be introduced as rapidly as possible throughout the organization. For example, there are a number of organizations conducting across-the-board "management-by-objectives" programs because the chief executive enthusiastically supports them. Frequently such total organization programs really do not improve the organization.

On balance, however, top management's active support and commitment to a program makes a significant difference in the predictability of its success. Assuming that significant organization development involves changes in values, norms, and perhaps goals, it is an essential condition that the chief executives be active in the process.

2. *The Unit Head.* Another way of starting a total organization development program arises out of a situation where a unit, perhaps a division or segment of a company, is headed by a person who becomes interested in and enthusiastic about a planned-change effort for his organization. If the unit he heads is relatively autonomous within the larger organization, he will be able to move ahead with an effective change effort. The results of this effort may well spread to other units of the organization. In one very large organization, a planned strategy of organization improvement in one division has produced quite dramatic results both in the profit figures in the financial statement, and in the general work climate of the

organization. This difference in performance and climate has become obvious to many people in the total organization, including key management at the headquarters. The top management, who previously were less committed to this type of planned change effort, have, from looking at the results, begun to reassess their own attitudes and are moving toward more organization-wide change efforts. They are also looking to other division efforts and are developing new criteria for measuring effective performance-improvement programs. Some of the advantages of this way of moving are:

a) The individual unit manager's performance usually looks better.

b) He probably will be seen as progressive and forward-looking and may be rewarded accordingly.

c) Such an effort also will tend to build more management strength into his own organization, thus freeing him up for promotion-availability possibilities.

d) It also provides a pilot model which may stimulate other efforts.

On the negative side, a unit engaging in any program which is very different from the norms of an organization may be seen as "way out" or deviant. There may be some envy and perhaps anger from other parts of the organization. There may be some form of boycotting of the "oddballs." There is always the possibility that, as a suborganization's way of work becomes more "open" and confronting, the members will practice this behavior in other settings; this may produce some difficulties in relationships with other groups. However, if there is enthusiastic effort by the head of the organization both to build his internal organization and to improve the relationships with other parts of the organization, an effective change program is likely to result.

3. *The Evangelist.* In every organization there are a few people (who may be located almost anywhere in the formal power structure), who are "natural leaders" and who have great influence on the total organization. Their official roles may not provide them with immediate control over numbers of people in the organization, but their power, stemming from their ability to influence significant people, may be more potent than official authority.

I know of several instances where such a person has been "turned on" by the possibilities of a planned effort to improve the organization's effectiveness and health. One example is in a large organization where there are a number of people whose official role is the facilitation of change efforts. They have been moderately effective in a number of subunits of the organization, but have had very limited effect on the real power structure. A couple of years ago, a person fairly high up in the organization and with influence considerably larger than his role, became "turned on" with the possibilities of this type of effort for the total organization. He had access to a number of key people throughout the organization where real changes were possible. He was able to go to a variety of strategic people and, because of the confidence they had in him, they were willing to engage in experimental activities. From these activities significant changes have occurred and some major programs have developed. An apt title for him, coined by one of those who responded to his efforts and whose organization is now much more effective, was "disciple in residence."

4. *The Functional Leader.* Another form of effort that can lead to large-system change efforts may start in the office of a functional head. One of the problems of complex organizations is that people performing specialized functions such as accounting, personnel, or management services, belong simultaneously to two organizations: the functional group and the administrative unit in which they are working. This overlapping membership produces a lot of problems in staff-line relationships, control, and career development, which get in the way of operating effectiveness.

I have seen several situations where the head of some staff function initiated a program of change with the line operators. (The case in Chapter 8 is one dramatic illustration of this form.) This mode requires a great deal of interpersonal competence and courage by the initiating director, and involves considerable confrontation of issues across lateral lines between staff and operating heads. It *can* end up producing new intergroup relationship problems. However, if it works effectively, it may well mobilize the entire organization toward a new mode of collaboration.

5. *The Convert Group.* One other condition that sometimes produces total organization change is where a group or subunit has had a particularly effective change experience, has seen results, and is convinced of the soundness of the effort. The group, using its own experience, tries to influence those parts of the organization with which it interfaces. The case in Chapter 7 illustrates this. In one of the large oil companies, a small group (which has had a major change program for themselves) has been

very effective in influencing organization improvement efforts in a number of other parts of the organization.

USE OF OUTSIDE HELP

It is important for change managers to understand the types of outside resources available, as well as the options for organizing the OD efforts within the organization. To help in thinking about this, I would like to discuss it in the following context. First, I will list a series of phases that are involved in any organization-wide change effort, thinking in terms of the total organization. Then I will look at types of arrangements between outside resources and organizations; and third, I will examine the relationship between these two. The purpose is to provide the reader with some criteria against which he can determine what type of outside help is most appropriate to what type of organization problem within his total OD effort.

Phases of Organization-wide Change Efforts

In a broad, general way, we can say that all OD efforts include the following processes:

> diagnosis,
> strategy planning,
> education,
> consulting and training,
> evaluation.

Diagnosis as used here means examining the need for change and the state of the system. *Strategy planning* refers to developing a plan for organization improvement, including the determination as to what systems are to be engaged and in what order, what activities should be initiated, what resources are needed. *Education* as used here implies those phases of organization development in which some part of the system, or parts of the system, are engaged in an effort which is primarily educational rather than action-oriented. This may be a "music appreciation" session with the top-management group where an outsider is talking about what kinds of activities are going on in other organizations. It may be attendance at a Managerial Grid seminar to understand the Grid OD program. It may be a series of presentations by experts in the field, describing what is possible in the way of improving organization effectiveness and coping. *Consulting* and *training* as used here refer to the consulting on present practices or planning for new practices either of the total system or of subgroups; training means the expert assistance in carrying out training activities which are part of the program. For example, if sensitivity-training programs are seen as part of an OD effort, there would be "trainers" required for such activities. If the organization is conducting a *Phase-One* Grid activity, there will be "trainers" involved. *Evaluating* as used here means the continuous evaluation of the effects of a change program on the total organization. What is the state of the organization's health? One model is to have an outside consultant come in once a year and help an organization "take its own temperature." The function of the outsider is to facilitate the data-collection and temperature-taking. Other models include attitude surveys, survey-feedback projects, research projects by behavioral scientists, and internal employee-relations research groups.

Types of Outside Resource "Contracts"

Following is a representative list of types of arrangements or "contracts" entered into between organizations and outside resources. The list is not all-inclusive, but it covers the major types. Let's look briefly at each of these arrangements.

1. *The Continuity Arrangement.* This is an arrangement whereby the outside consultant is on some form of retainer to either the total system or a significant part of it. He spends time on a regular basis, say two or three days a month, in the organization. His specific activities are programmed jointly with the OD management within the organization, and are determined by the ongoing problems in the system. For example, he may attend staff meetings; he may provide individual consultation to a number of executives; he may sit in as a catalyst between two groups. He is a continuing, though part time, member of a change team. In this role he needs considerably more orientation and knowledge about the organization and its activities than would be true if he were functioning in one of the other types of relationships to be described.

2. *The Periodic Review.* There is an arrangement between the consultant and the organization for him to visit it on a regular and periodic basis for

the purpose of helping the organization examine its own functioning, processes, and effectiveness. This can take several forms.

For example, I have had such arrangements with organizations whereby I would visit with a management committee three or four times a year, spending a day with them on their own functioning and helping them in the definition of key problems in the organization. Another arrangement provides for the consultant to help the organization do a "total temperature-taking" through a confrontation meeting or through a series of interviews of strategic people followed by a feedback session.

Another type of arrangement is to have a behavioral-science research team come into the organization and do a study using survey methods, with feedback to the appropriate parts of the organization. In this arrangement, the primary functions of the outside resource are two: one, to collect information and feed it back; and the other, to assist parts of the organization in the processes of diagnosis and action-planning. The consultant needs to know a moderate amount about the organization. His interventions or consultive activities are likely to consist mainly of making sure that the client organization has adequate information and looks at it and does its own planning.

3. *The Project Arrangement.* In this mode, the relationship between the organization and the outside help is more that of the client-expert type, although many of the activities performed may well be more consultative than expert. Here the organization brings in outside help to assist with the management of a particular program or project.

An example is the start-up of a new plant or operation. In such a situation there are a number of unique relationships and processes which occur only during the beginning of an organization's life. Behavioral-science knowledge and technology are used in such situations to help with the development of new management teams, the setting up of temporary planning organizations, and the reduction of potential intergroup problems (between, for example, the new operating team and the corporate engineering or planning team who set up the project).

Under another kind of a project arrangement, a consultant is called in to help an organization work on the problems of introducing a computer into an organization. The development and monitoring of a program for dealing with the human factors might be a specific project.

A third example would be the problems involved in a merger between either subunits of a large organization or between organizations. The many human factors and communications problems that exist in such situations can be worked with, and the problems reduced, by the application of behavioral-science knowledge and technology. A number of organizations turn to outside help in this type of situation.

A fourth illustration is a situation where an organization is introducing a new management practice or program, such as an individual-performance improvement program, sometimes called target setting or "management by objectives." The organization may turn to outside help for the education of its leadership at various levels, and for the installation of the program throughout various levels of the organization. Here the arrangement between the organization and the outside help is for the installation of a specific program. There are a number of consulting organizations in the United States and Europe that specialize in this type of program installation. In this kind of arrangement, the "contract" has pretty specific boundaries—the project is fairly clearly defined. It is therefore not necessary for the consultant to know as much about the organization and its people as would be required in the previous arrangements. In this mode the consultant brings expertise and experience with a particular application which can be adapted to the specifics of the client organization.

4. *Educational Consultation.* A number of companies will turn to a university-based behavioral scientist or to a consultant to provide educational counseling and information on the state of the art for some part of their executive group. This arrangement may take several forms.

a)   The "music appreciation" style. In this situation, the educational "expert" makes a presentation, formal or informal, to the top management of the organization, or to a selected group of key executives. Such a presentation might describe what is going on in the use of applied behavioral science today; explain what organization development is and how it is being used; or illustrate trends in management development. The use of behavioral-science consultants in this way has increased markedly in the last couple of years. This device is being used more and more frequently by staff people in an organization as a "softening up" of line executives.

b)   The "in-house" seminar. In this form, the staff organization brings educational resources to the organization's headquarters on a systematic basis. It's the "mountain goes to Mohammed" theory. A number of the largest American corporations run continuous schools for middle and upper-middle management, at which a parade of experts and consultants appears, each discoursing on his own specialty. The management is thus exposed to a fairly extensive survey course on the state of the art.

c)   The "dog and pony show." In this mode, a number of organizations will arrange some "big name" attractions in the field to give a lecture or evening presentation to selected executives from a number of organizations in a community. This pattern is one of "performance," where a presentation is given by the "outsider" and follow-up is done by local people in the home setting.

I have categorized this type of arrangement separately because, as one of many organization-development strategies, it is becoming a familiar enough phenomenon to merit the attention of interested managers. Obviously in this type of relationship relatively little information about the specific organization is required by the expert.

5. *The Trainer Arrangement.* In this arrangement the organization hires outside help to do a specific type of training activity. An example would be sensitivity trainers. A number of organizations conduct in-company sensitivity-training activities for which they hire outside behavioral-science consultants. These consultants serve as faculty.

A number of package programs require outside help to conduct the original program, and then use the outside help to train in-company specialists to conduct the programs within the organization.

6. *The Packaged OD Program.* In this arrangement, the organization commits itself to a particular set of organization-development procedures. The most popular, and one of the most effective, of these integrated program efforts is the previously mentioned Managerial Grid OD program. In this type of relationship, the company, on a planned basis, sends people through an educational phase, a team-building and development phase, a phase dealing with intergroup relationships, and a goal-setting and planning phase. Outside help is used in terms of strategy planning; in conducting pilot runs; in training trainers for follow-up activities; and for quality control of some of the educational activities. A number of multiphase programs which can be applied organization-wide have emerged in the last few years. The manager planning a development effort should be aware of these. In this type of relationship the amount of knowledge of the specific

company required by the outside help is minimal. The program brings a set of tested methods and processes which, on a "self-help" basis, can be applied by the membership of the organization itself.

7. *The Consulting Team.* One type of arrangement that is used by a few companies is the employment of a *team* of outside resources. This pattern is applicable only in a relatively complex organization. In cases where it has proved effective, there are a number of consultants, each one assigned to a particular subsector of the organization and preferably paired with an inside consultant. The group of consultants meets with key line and staff people for organization-wide strategy planning, quality control, and temperature-taking. An application of this mode is described in more detail in Sheldon Davis' article in the *Journal of Applied Behavioral Science.*[1]

In this situation, understanding the organization culture, goals, and norms, is very important. The amount of briefing and updating required between the organization and consultants is relatively large.

8. *The Organization-wide Evaluation.* I list this as a pattern in itself because there are a number of cases in large multinational or multi-industry companies where the management of the organization has entered into a relationship with outside behavioral scientists with the specific purpose of doing a study of the organization system, its effectiveness, its norms, and its culture. An extensive study has recently been completed in one of the largest oil companies, in which the total system in ten different countries was studied against a particular model of managerial systems and strategies. In another large oil company, a contract was entered into to examine the total organization in terms of employee commitment to organization-mission objectives. Large organizations, which have engaged in a number of organization-development efforts with subunits of the organization, may employ outside help to make a comparison study of the different types of efforts. This is a relatively specialized arrangement, but it has occurred enough times that it should be borne in mind by managers concerned with the total spectrum of possibilities.

1   Davis, S. A. "An Organic Problem-Solving Method of Organizational Change." *Journal of Applied Behavioral Science,* 1967, 3, No. 1, 3-21.

Relationship of Arrangements to Change Processes

The chart (see Fig. 10.1) illustrates generally the connection between the type of arrangement or relationship between the organization and its outside help, and the processes of organization improvement to which the help is applied.

1. The continuity arrangement tends to be involved with diagnosis, strategy planning, education, consulting and training, and evaluation.

2. The periodic-review arrangement tends to deal with diagnosis, strategy planning, and some evaluation.

3. The project arrangement tends to be concerned with strategy planning, education, and consulting and training.

4. The educational-consultant situation tends to deal with education, and perhaps with diagnosis.

5. The packaged OD program tends to deal with education, consulting and training, and occasionally some strategy planning.

6. The consulting-team mode deals with diagnosis, strategy planning, and perhaps some education.

7. The organization-evaluation or research arrangement deals with diagnosis and evaluation.

INSIDE CHANGE AGENTS

Let's look now at some of the ways staff help is mobilized and organized within organizations.

1. *The Organization-Development Department.* Some organizations set up a department in the corporate center, usually reporting either to the vice-president of industrial relations or of human resources, or to the president, called an organization-development or organization-improvement department. This department frequently functions as an internal consulting organization available, on call, to various segments of the organization to help them with diagnosis, strategy planning, and the conduct of various types of programs.

Relationship	Diagnosis	Strategy planning	Education	Consulting and training	Organization evaluation
Continuity	X	X	X	X	X
Periodic review	X	X			X
Project	X	X	X		
Educational consultant		X	X		
Trainer			X	X	
Packaged organizational development program		X	X	X	
Consulting team	X	X	X		
Organization evaluator	X				X

Fig. 10.1 Outside Help and Change Processes

The strengths of this plan are that it brings together a few specialists who are highly tuned to the state of the art and are in touch with the entire field. The weakness of this organization is that it tends to locate the specialty in a staff department frequently disconnected from the rest of the personnel and human-resources functions. Over an extended period of time, this arrangement may isolate, and increase the distance between, the various parts of the organization concerned with the human factors, and can end up in overcentralization of the resource and a lack of line "ownership in" the program.

However, if properly connected to the rest of the organization, a small organization-development department can be a very effective central-staff resource.

2. *The Organization-Development Specialist.* This is a situation where a person or persons are attached to either the top of the personnel organization or the top of the line organization, again functioning as internal consultants. They are identified as resource specialists to assist in identifying planned-change problems and working the problems. The person functions very much as an outside consultant and referral source. He may do a limited number of training activities, but is more likely to

function as a catalyst. In one large company this function is called behavioral-sciences applications. The person in this role has complete freedom to move throughout the organization to facilitate change efforts. He may work with any part of the organization that has a change problem. It is also his responsibility to be tuned in to the latest theory and practice in applied behavioral science. In this role he has access to professional resources all over the world. One of his main functions is to bring resources together with ready clients.

This mode has some advantages over the more formal organization-development department, in that it provides specialist help but does not develop a piece of organization structure which requires organizations to refer to organizations. Rather, those wanting help can call on an individual who can either provide it or refer the client to appropriate resources.

3. *The Personnel Man with Organization Development as His Primary Job.* Numbers of organizations are restructuring the functions within the personnel department. For example, one "design" divides the total set of personnel functions into three categories. One category deals with the "contract" between the individual and the organization and includes recruitment, employment, training, job enlargement, some parts of career development, compensation, and separation. A second category has to do with information flow, including such things as management inventory, record-keeping, and publications. A third category has to do with organization development. This involves such activities as team-development, goal-setting, and planning. This third category works with groups within the organization.

There seems to be a trend, where this mode is followed, for the *top* man in the personnel or human resources area to take on this third category himself and to assign the first two categories to other managers in his department.

The advantage of this mode is that it keeps the OD function connected with the other aspects of human-resources management. It also defines the emphasis and priority attached to the organization-development efforts since the top man takes this on as his personal area of concern.

4. *The "Account Executive."* This term, borrowed from the advertising field, is used to denote a form of management of the staff effort that one finds in some large, decentralized organizations. In this mode, people in some aspect of the personnel function in the headquarters, (for example, employee relations) are assigned a number of field locations, such as

plants, where they are the "headquarters men" for those locations. Each of them is the account executive for a plant (or plants). Their primary mission is to work as a consultant to the unit management in diagnosis of the health and the needs of the organization, and to identify and secure appropriate resources from the center of the organization and from outside. The advantage of this arrangement is that it provides a broadened base of help for the unit management and does a lot to improve headquarters/field relationships by improved communication between the field units and the headquarters through the "friend" or account executive at headquarters.

5. *The "Temporary" Change Agent.* In several large organizations, experiments are being conducted in taking people from line positions, identifying them as organization-change agents and assigning them specific "clients" with whom they work for a period of a year or so. During the time they are employed as "change agents" or "consultants," they get special training in change technology, organization dynamics and organization development. Some of the thinking behind this type of arrangement is that when such people return to their line positions they are much better equipped and ready to take on change-management *assignments.* Several organizations where this has been tried have reported quite favorable results.

6. *The Training Consultant.* This is a role, usually found in a headquarters, which is an extension of the traditional training-director role. This person is seen as someone who can help with group and intergroup training activities, such as team-development programs, intergroup workshops, goal-setting programs, etc. He is an internal consultant on those types of organization-improvement efforts involving groups or groups of groups.

7. *The Grid Organization-Development Coordinator.* This is a person, from either a staff or a line position, who functions as the internal coordinator during an organization-wide Grid OD program. It is his job to arrange the various activities, to consult with the various family-group leaders, to sit in as appropriate during team-development programs, to advise the top management on progress in the total strategy, and to provide periodic evaluation of the program.

8. *The "New Look" Management-Development Department.* Perhaps the most common mode is where the management-development department

has taken on additional responsibilities. In addition to their work with individual managers on selection, training, and rotation, they become the home of the resources for team development, manpower planning, and other organization-improvement activities.

There is a logic to the extension of management-development specialists into organization-development resources. The difficulty arises when the change of role is perceived as different by other parts of the organization. There are today a number of in-house development programs for management-development people toward the end of building this technology into existing management-development departments.

SUMMARY

In this chapter we have examined some of the types of change management and change assistants which seem to be appropriate in organization-development efforts in terms of line management, the use of outside help, and the organization of internal-staff resources.

In the final chapter we will look at what seems to lie ahead in the next few years as the major themes attached to systematic organization improvement.

11

THE THEME OF THE SEVENTIES

In Chapter 1, I reviewed briefly some of the high points in management's continuing search for the excellent organization. We looked at the progression of the themes in this century from the focus on human engineering, to the focus on human relations, to the heavy emphasis on manager development in the fifties, and then on to the current theme of organization development.

In Chapters 2 to 10, we have looked in detail at organization development as a phenomenon, and its relationship to management-development training and operations research. We have examined the characteristics and components of organization-development efforts and strategies; we have looked at a series of actual cases of organization-development efforts and at the management and staffing of organization development.

This brings us to what I believe is the inevitable conclusion as to the underlying theme of the seventies: the *"active and continuing search for organization excellence."*

It is not necessary to have a crystal ball to see the trends for the next few years in organization-improvement efforts. These trends have already started and are the subject of much thought and concern, today, both in firms and in organization management, and in the university faculties who are preparing organization managers for the future. I would like to briefly discuss what I think are several major trends which will be part of our organizational life in the next decade.

1. *Close Linkage in the Teaching of Management Sciences and Behavioral Sciences in Management Schools.*[1] I believe that in the years ahead there will be a new fusion of effort between those who are trying to prepare managers for organization leadership through the teaching of better decision-making methods and information analysis and use, and those who are trying to prepare managerial talent to be able to optimize the creativity and potential of the human resources in the organization. Today, these subjects are taught quite independently, with very little connection between the subjects and the teachers. The student has to figure out the possible connections between the two, which may seem to be in direct conflict with each other. I think we will see more integration in this teaching. We will see more vertical courses—different disciplines brought together around this subject area. For example, there may be courses on the "problems of introducing a new technology," including both the technology and the behavioral consequences of its introduction.

2. *A Heavy Focus on Integrating Theory and Practice in Management-School Curricula.* I believe that in the years to come we will see more emphasis on behavioral-science applications and much more experience-based training. There is already significant evidence of this trend at a number of leading management schools, such as the Harvard Business School, Columbia School of Business, UCLA Graduate School of Business Administration, and the Sloan School of Management at Massachusetts Institute of Technology. For example, at MIT, we have developed a "track" for our Masters' students in management; in this program, a student getting his degree in management can choose all his electives in his two years to focus on organization development. He takes courses in planned change, organization diagnosis, managerial behavior; he has field experience, working on organization development in a company, and he writes his thesis in this field. However, he graduates with a degree in management, having had a full management course.

3. *The "Management of Change" as a Part of all Management Training.* I believe that educational programs inside and outside companies will have a major focus on education in the management of change. This will be considered an essential part of the basic skills and abilities required for anyone in management.

---

1   For further detail see "From Confusion to Fusion: Integrating Our Educational and Managerial Efforts," by Richard Beckhard. Douglas McGregor Memorial Lecture, Cambridge, Mass.: M.I.T., Oct. 10, 1968.

4. *Emergence of a "Profession" of Change Agents.* I believe we are beginning to see the emergence of a professional person whose career interest is in the facilitation of organization change and improvement. The technical background for such a person will include knowledge and skill in the behavioral sciences and the management sciences, as well as the problems of enterprise management. His background will include work in organization diagnosis, and he will have high interpersonal competence, skills in problem-solving, change methods, consultation, and training. He will be a specialist in understanding human processes, with an orientation toward collaborative inquiry.

5. *Better Integration of Specialties in the Firm.* I believe we will see considerable movement toward more collaboration, and perhaps we will see structural reorganization among the specialists in the management of behavioral sciences in the firm. Whereas, today, specialists in these two fields operate independently of each other and are rewarded for their effectiveness in introducing their specialty into the organization, I suspect that in the years ahead we will find more and more efforts toward collaboration between these two specialties; and the organization will reward participants who contribute to the total improvement of the organization and the integration of the two areas of knowledge in organization improvement.

For example, in one large chemical company today, it is standard practice that whenever a "client" line or staff organization calls on either the management services or the organization-development group for consultation, the other specialty is brought in at the problem-diagnosis stage. The client is always exposed to this broader range of potential help. In the future we may well see these two specialist functions reporting to the same top vice-president, who will be heading a function that might be called organization change or organization planning.

6. *Organization Leaders Will Be* Explicit *in Stating both* Value *Aims and Goals and* Financial and Market *Aims and Goals.* Top management will be more and more articulate and explicit about the kind of environment and the kind of values about people and their work that should pertain in their organizations. Programs of improvement will be aimed toward, and measured against, these explicit goals.

Some companies have already begun to formulate corporate-objectives statements. The following are two examples.

1. "The company aims to be a successful business which lives out its concern for the dignity and worth of its members as it pursues profits. To accomplish this, the company will attempt to operate in such a way as to:

accept people as they are,

expect responsible behavior,

support individuals and personal growth,

assist individuals to develop their competencies,

enlarge the opportunity for impact of each individual in the company in every practical way,

bend every effort to resolve conflicts through discussions and fair judgment, minimizing arbitrary rules and use of authority."

2. "We have two basic aims: One is to make products which are genuinely new and useful to the public, products of the highest quality and at reasonable cost. In this way we assure the financial success of the company and each of us has the satisfaction of helping to make a creative contribution to the society. The other is to give everyone working for the company a personal opportunity within the company for full exercise of his talents: to express his opinions, to share in the progress of the company as far as his capacities permit, to earn enough money so that the need for earning more will not always be the first thing on his mind—opportunity, in short, to make his work here a fully rewarding and important part of his life."

If these trends do continue, and I predict they will, top managements will organize to achieve both high-performance objectives and the values stated in the above two examples. A significant aspect of the theme of the seventies *"the active and continuing search for excellence"*—will be an organization climate in which people can grow and develop, in which creative capacity can be unleashed, and in which people's personal needs for moving toward their own potential can be significantly achieved in the work setting.